Over to you Richie

First published in 1993 by
Swan Publishing Pty Ltd
P.O. Box 577, Nedlands, W.A. 6009

Copyright © 1993
Swan Publishing Ltd

National Library of Australia
Cataloguing-in-Publication data.

Over to you Richie.

ISBN 0 646 14642 4.

1. Cricket 2. Cricket players – Anecdotes.
3. Sportscasters – Anecdotes.

796.358

Printed in Australia by McPherson's Printing Group

Editor: Dawn Cockle
Contributing Editor: John Benaud
Designer: Stan Lamond, Lamond Art & Design
Statistics: Ross Dundas

Over to you Richie

Classics from the Captains of Commentary

Cartoons by
Jeff Hook

SWAN
PUBLISHING

Contents

Part One

Part Two

Part One

Introduction

"Now it's over to Richie Benaud in the central commentary position ..." They're the words cricket fans hear a hundred times a summer, the signal that play is about to get underway in any one of the Tests or World Series matches covered by Nine's *Wide World of Sports*.

Nine's cricket coverage has brought a new appreciation of the oldest game: precise camerawork that grabs the viewer and sits him on the edge of his loungechair, expert commentary from a team of highly respected cricketers, all of whom achieved the ultimate honour the game can offer, to captain his country.

Yet all the viewer really knows about the members of the team is, in the case of the commentators, either the history of their cricketing careers, or what they see and hear via the television. And they know nothing at all about the people behind the scenes.

This book lets on a little bit more about them all: revealed is the dry, but very funny sense of humour of the silver-haired Richie Benaud, the odd cooking crisis as well as some pertinent thoughts on just where the game is heading as a new century approaches.

Ian Chappell had a reputation as a mighty tough cricketer. Just how tough? Well, not even brotherly love saved the day following the dramatic Underarm incident. Yet there is a marvellous biting humour to Chappell that many will appreciate, even if they do find it hard to equate with those always so-serious features.

Naturally, there are some 'classics' from Bill Lawry, whose nickname by the way is 'The Phantom', earned because of his love for that particular comic book in his youth. The high-pitched tone of his television commentary is muted in this book, but that is not to say his views are not forthright, clear and definitely valuable input for any thinking cricket administrators. And he lets viewers into a few secrets about racing pigeons!

Tony Greig, trivia buffs will be delighted to know, is the tallest cricketer ever to represent England. And they can also find out about all those 'national identity' hassles that go on during telecasts between Tony, Ian Chappell and Bill Lawry.

Every cricket fan concedes Greg Chappell was among the greatest players of all time, yet his career was dogged by the controversy of the infamous underarm delivery. What happened to make Greg order his younger brother Trevor to bowl that ball? For the first time Greg talks about the mental pressures he felt in the game at that time.

Which brings us to David Gower. It's impossible to imagine pressure and Gower ever coming together, so delightfully relaxed does he always look when he graces a cricket field. Bill Lawry says when Gower goes in to bat the bars empty out. But there is so much more to Gower than his cricket—African safaris and tobogganing are just two.

The member of the cricket team viewers never see is its skipper, Brian C Morelli. But the Nine telecast without 'BC' would be just like the Australian batting order without 'AB'.

The Skipper

You won't find the name Brian C Morelli listed anywhere in the 'bible' of cricketers, *Wisden*. In fact, the only times Morelli may have put bat to ball were possibly in the backyard at his mum's.

But Morelli has the runs on the board, so to speak, when it comes to putting the Test cricket, and one-day cricket, into loungerooms around Australia, indeed around the world.

Brian C Morelli is the executive director of the Nine television network's *Wide World of Sports*.

His critics have adjudged his work well: there have been numerous Logie awards for the cricket coverage, Penguin awards for his direction of the Formula One motor racing grand prix, four Confederation of Motor Sport awards for Formula One coverage, and Penguin commendation awards for Rugby League telecasts.

Super scoreboard that!

No wonder he's 'captain of the captains', the man whose television tactics help make Richie Benaud, Ian Chappell, Tony Greig, Bill Lawry, David Gower and Greg Chappell such a formidable team of cricket commentators.

B C MORELLI

"Television will not last, it's a flash in the pan." So said A J Knight, chief designing engineer of the Metropolitan Water Sewerage and Drainage Board in Sydney. "I've seen it overseas and it doesn't impress me." Knight was speaking to Brian C Morelli, who was standing before him with his resignation in his hand. It was July 1956. Morelli had earlier that year returned to the Photographic Section of the Board after completing his national service in the Royal Australian Air Force.

In spite of the warning he resigned and started at TCN Channel Nine, Sydney, on August 13, 1956 to inaugurate the film department.

On opening night of television, September 16, 1956, he was in the theatrette, which was doubling as a studio, when Bruce Gyngell said, "Good evening, and welcome to television."

From then on it was a reasonably rapid rise through the studio ranks to become a director. Morelli was on the production team of programmes which introduced to TV audiences Jimmy Hannan, Reg Grundy, Brian Henderson, Roger Climpson, Bob Rogers and many others.

In 1977 he teamed up with David Hill, who came to the Nine Network as executive producer of sport. It has since been hailed as the most successful team in television production of sport ever seen in Australia.

World Series Cricket was then created. "I don't know if we were created as a team for it or it was created for us. I do know it was a perfect vehicle for us."

The television coverage created during those early years is still the format used today. It is also the same format used by all of the cricketing television broadcasters around the world. Although a lot of refinements have been added over the years by Morelli, he says most viewers wouldn't be able to pick them out. However one such invention does indeed stand out: it is stump-vision.

Stump-vision is a miniature camera inserted in a cricket stump and it allows the viewers to see an angle as if they were sitting directly behind the batsman.

Warren Berkery deserves praise as well, Morelli says. "You can have as many ideas as you like, but if you don't have a skilled production and technical crew you might as well put your idea on paper, put it in a bottle and throw it in the ocean." Berkery worked on the technical requirements to fit the mini-camera into the stump.

The cricket telecast is the most successful sporting programme in the country. It has been a great stepping stone from which production skills have been taken and used on other major products.

Morelli hopes to make further advancement in cricket as more and more technology based on miniature cameras comes onto the market. "I see a time when we will be able to have miniature cameras on players and quite possibly in the pitch."

The Team

By B C Morelli

RICHIE BENAUD

I'm not sure whether we joined Richie or Richie joined us when World Series Cricket was created in 1977. Whichever it was, Richie was already a very impressive and experienced broadcaster. His eye for detail and his memory bank were both the mainstay of our broadcast format.

I listened intently during those early days to everything he said. His "I remember when" stories of the most detailed cricketing situations were bordering on incredible.

Over the years I also learnt that he possesses a wonderful sophisticated sense of humour. Many an example of this was performed on air, the least of which he repeated many times before my wife pointed it out to me. It happened when he was referring to the wicket report. He would work into his remarks the phrase "there was a lot of sweating under the covers last night".

One time during a Test match in Adelaide there was a quiet period of play after lunch. To help kick along the telecast I took sequences of spectators in various array. Having witnessed both sides of Richie, I should have been prepared for what followed, but alas I wasn't.

One sequence was of people wearing unusual hats. Richie made a very descriptive commentary over the pictures. One

13

of the shots was of a man in a deerstalker hat. Richie asked if he could see that shot again and added, "That fellow in the deerstalker, could I see him again? I think he is ..." Before he finished I jumped in and said, "I don't want to take the shot by itself. I will have to make it part of a group again."

In between deliveries in the game I organised the cameras to frame their shots to suit the sequence. As some of the cameras that had found good subjects would also be covering play, I had to have those pictures videotaped.

All the time I was organising this Richie kept inquiring about our progress on another viewing of 'deerstalker'.

Eventually, after organising a rather complicated sequence of pictures, some live, some from videotape, I was ready. "Here we go Richie" I announced proudly.

As the sequence went to air the 'deerstalker' was strategically placed to allow Richie time to identify him and elaborate over the remaining pictures ... but there was silence.

After the sequence finished Richie called down to me on the lazy mike and said, "Thanks BC, never saw him before in my life."

BILL LAWRY

Bill Lawry's love and enthusiasm for cricket boils over into his commentary. Bill's main aim is to keep the viewer informed and entertained. Bill is a director's dream. He loves calling for close-ups of players, on-screen information, replays and so on.

To do this there is a microphone in the commentary position which is called the 'lazy mike'. Commentators hold the on-air microphone in one hand and pick up the lazy mike to speak to the director with requests that the viewer doesn't hear. Naturally you must remove the on-air mike away from your mouth to speak into the 'lazy'.

During a World Series Cup final, Australia needed to win to take the prize. Australia was fielding. The batting side needed 50 runs and had five wickets in hand. The pressure was starting to build. One wicket fell, then shortly after, another. Twenty runs had been added.

Bill was now almost at boiling point. "Lillee comes storming in. He's overstepped. No-ball."

Grabbing the lazy mike he said "Replay." The replay was put to air. "Oh dear, Australia can't afford too many of

those." Bill cried, "Just twenty runs to get now, three wickets remaining."

Bill called for a close-up of Rodney Marsh. "There goes the secret signal from Marsh to Lillee. In he comes again, the greatest bowler in the world. Oh, beautiful ball. No run."

Bill called again on the lazy, "Replay," and then again, "Close-up of Dennis please."

As Dennis was running in Bill started what was to become one of the funniest scenes I have ever witnessed in television.

Bill: "Two balls to go, this one should be a yorker ... yes! Got him. He's out. Lillee's done it." Picking up the lazy mike he said "Replay!" and then continued his comments into the lazy mike. "Lillee has removed the last decent batsman. Australia should now go on to win it. Look at this delivery. He kept it up. The batsman had nowhere to go, the perfect yorker. What a delivery, what a bowler!"

Into his on-air mike he said, "Another replay please." He then returned to the lazy mike and continued his commentary. "Lillee may have lost a little pace but he hasn't lost any of the ability."

Again on the on-air mike he said, "Close-up of the new batsman please."

Continuing on the lazy mike he said, "These are the bunnies now, the tail-enders."

By now we had all stopped laughing and re-gathered our senses. Bill was still going hammer and tongs into the lazy.

"Bill, Bill," I said. "Stop. Would you please tell the viewers what is happening, and not tell me. I can see it!"

IAN CHAPPELL

I have never told 'Chappelli' this story and I probably shouldn't commit it to publication either, as the theory of the story couldn't be further from the truth. Anyhow here goes.

Some years ago a match at Brisbane finished early. The commentators and I found ourselves sitting out at the airport waiting for the earliest flight home.

The inevitable happened—the commentators started talking cricket. The subject centred around English players. I was fascinated to observe that when talking of cricketers they invariably describe them as 'the leggie', 'the offie', 'the quickie' and so on. Names don't come into it.

Associated with this are hand gestures which relate to the method bowlers use to release the ball. When speaking about batsmen they hold their hand with the palm facing their body, elbow bent at a right angle and fingers pointed down. The hand is moved away from the body as if playing a shot. An exaggerated movement of the hand toward or away from the face denotes that you played a cramped-up shot on the back foot or used your feet forward.

When describing bowlers their hand, limp wrist and arm, start in a shape which doesn't look unlike a swan's head and neck. When you speak about a 'quickie', a fast motion is made, almost as a swan would do if lunging for something in the water.

It looks particularly suspicious when the person is describing a spin bowler delivering a flipper which comes out of the back of the hand. It must look even worse when you cannot hear the conversation. It happened that way in England in 1989.

Ian Chappell had stopped to talk to an English friend. I strolled on and stopped about 10 metres further on. By his actions I could see Chappelli was discussing a 'leggie'.

However, a Yorkshire cricket fan stopped just near me and spied Ian talking to his acquaintance. He stood in silence for a short time observing the 'swan' actions and then said, "Bloody 'ell! I would never have believed it, if I 'adn't seen it with my own eyes."

TONY GREIG

The banter that exists between Tony Greig and Bill Lawry concerning any Australia versus England match is now legendary. Tony has never forgotten his mother country ties when such a contest takes place. To this day he remains ever so faithful.

There was a Test, though, that really tested his mettle. It was the Second Test at Brisbane in the 1982–83 Ashes series. Australia was performing well. From memory Kepler Wessels made a century on debut, Rod Marsh reached the unique total of 300 catches and set an Ashes record by holding six in an innings. He also equalled a record of nine in a match.

Bill, of course, was going for the jugular, aided and abetted by my good self. As a director on the cricket telecasts I have an open microphone to the commentators. They hear all of the directions to cameramen and the crew and to the videotape operators who control the replays.

Much was made of Tony Greig's height of 6 feet 7½ inches (375 centimetres), the rakish angle at which he wore his cap, not unlike a soldier of the American civil war, and his aggressive streak when he made his Test debut against Ian Chappell's Australian team in the First Test at Old Trafford in 1972. Greig made 57 and 62, top score in both innings.

Naturally it allows me to have a three-way conversation with the commentators without my part of the conversation going to air.

Bill and I were having a field day at Tony's expense about how good the Aussie team was performing. Their success just kept rolling along, and when Geoff Lawson became the first bowler to take 11 wickets in an Ashes Test at Brisbane, and Australia were the first side to hold 19 catches in a Test, Bill erupted. "It's all happening here at the Gabba." The favourite Lawry cliché was an understatement.

Greig, having been battered by Bill on air and being battered by me in his ear, was crestfallen. He gathered all his diminishing commentary power and said, "You must remember Bill, England on this tour is without Graham Gooch, Geoff Boycott, Mike Gatting, Peter Willey, Chris Old, John Emburey, Alan Knott, Mike Brearley, and of course Dilley."

Before Bill could get a word out, I replied into Tony's ear with, "... and you would still have W G Grace too, except that he died!"

Tony laughingly said, on air, "Fair enough."

Bill just laughed. I'm sure the viewers didn't have a clue what had transpired.

Australia went on to win that series, Tony.

GREG CHAPPELL

I suppose Greg Chappell would like to think that a quick spray from his favourite personal deodorant would get rid of the odour from his underarm problem. The slogan "Even your best friends won't tell you" didn't work here. One of his best friends did tell him. Rod Marsh, the Australian wicketkeeper in the match, said, "No don't do it."

The television commentary box was aghast. The whole cricketing world were eventually aghast. The headlines that followed the incident probably made Gregory Stephen Chappell aghast as well.

In my opinion, if history is going to remember you it will be for something people can get their teeth into, not just the fact that you scored a lot of runs. People speak of Don Bradman's highest score of 452, but how many will remember the 333 Graham Gooch scored without having to refer to *Wisden*?

For instance, do you remember the name of the first Irishman who starved himself to death in protest against the British rule in Northern Ireland? Do you remember the name of the man who shot and killed Robert Kennedy? Do you remember the name of the umpire standing during the underarm delivery? They are all part of history but few recall them.

Once I was lunching with John Bertrand soon after he skippered Australia's win of the America's Cup yacht race.

I told him not to defend the next challenge. "You will live longer in history as the first person to win it in 132 years than if you won it and then lost it next time round." I don't know if he took my advice but he didn't defend the title.

Now back to G S Chappell. I tsk-ed tsk-ed along with everybody else when it happened, until the New Zealand prime minister got involved.

Prime Minister Muldoon, when making his observation of the incident, said in part (referring to the World Series coloured clothing, which for Australia is green and gold, or 'yellow'), "The colour of the Australian uniform is perfect for the team."

I immediately stopped tsk-ing and started referring to Greg Chappell as 'Killer'. I would request of my cameramen during a telecast to give me a shot of 'Killer'. They would ask "Who's Killer?" and I'd reply, "Greg Chappell." Why do you call him 'Killer'? I was asked. Remembering the great Chappell family attitude of 'Go out there and win', I answered, "To win this series you have to have the killer instinct. Use all that is within the rules to achieve success."

Soon the crew all accepted master batsman Gregory Stephen Chappell, captain of Australia, as 'Killer'.

Low and behold it wasn't long before a couple of the commentators, during that season, also referred to him as 'Killer'. To this day, whenever I greet him I always say, "Gidday Killer."

DAVID GOWER

David Gower is a wag. The perpetual smiling eyes have a twinkle which lets you know he enjoys a joke.

David has only recently joined us. Our telecasts have developed over the years into a pretty solid format. Part of this established format are nicknames for computer information. These names allow us to talk in short-hand when requesting graphs and other computer-generated on-screen information.

The batting chart of a batsman shows the run-scoring strokes he has made. This is called the 'Wagon Wheel', as the lines within the perimeter of the cricket ground oval make the whole thing look like spokes within a wheel.

The graph which depicts the run rate of both teams in a one-day match looks like a worm, so I called it 'the Worm'. Others are called 'Calgary', 'Skyline', 'Bars', and 'Double Up'. All of these are used for the one-day matches.

Being a new commentator, David obviously had a lot of catching up to do in relation to nicknames. While on air one day he called down on the lazy mike, "Could I see the comparison graph please?"

> *David Gower captained England in 32 Tests, won five, lost 18 and drew nine. His loss record is the most by an England captain—but he did encounter the West Indies at their peak.*

I replied, "Do you want the Worm or Calgary?"

"I would like the one which shows the comparison between two batsmen."

"You want Double Up then," I said.

David said thoughtfully, "I rather fancied it was called Bars."

"No, Bars shows the runs per over as a single graph. Do you want to see the straight line or peaks?"

By now that twinkle in the eye was probably at its brightest. Almost with an exasperated reply he said, "Can I have them all up together and I'll pick the one I want."

Part Two

Chapter One

Richie Benaud

Born 1930, Richie Benaud. He started his first-class career with New South Wales when he was only 18 years old, then played his first Test for Australia against Jeff Stollmeyer's West Indies touring team in 1951–52. He was just 21, and described as a "promising leg-spin bowler".

It was the Fifth Test of the series and Australia won by 202 runs. The player Benaud today remembers as his favourite, Keith Miller, was mainly responsible for the West Indies scoring only 78 in their first innings, still their lowest against Australia. Miller took 5/26 off 7.6 overs—they were eight-ball overs in those days.

Benaud bowled only 4.3 overs in the match, in the second innings, and took 1/14. His first Test wicket was the bespectacled No. 11, Alf Valentine (batting average of 4.70 in Tests). An inauspicious start, but ...

He went on to take 248 Test wickets, which remained the record for any Australian bowler until the great Dennis Lillee had India's Chetan Chauhan caught by Bruce Yardley at the Melbourne Cricket Ground in 1981.

By the end of his career Benaud had become a household name, admired not just for his inspirational cricket, but for the positive manner in which he demanded the players under him play the game. He captained Australia to five successive winning series, against England twice, Frank Worrell's West Indians, India in India, and Pakistan in Pakistan.

Now, 30 years after he played his last Test, he is widely regarded as the game's shrewdest observer.

Tall and rangy, with a flowing gait, Benaud will be remembered as a hard-hitting, yet thoughtful lower-order batsman, but mainly as a crafty leg-spin bowler. His guile was such that at the end of his career he could literally run in blindfolded and still drop the ball on a good length!

He was an agile slips fieldsman, and his falling, left-handed catch of England's Colin Cowdrey at Lord's in 1956 was called "The Catch of the Century", although these days Bill Lawry would simply shout, "What a classic!"

Benaud is best remembered as the captain who, with the late Sir Frank Worrell, his opposite in the 1961 series with the West Indies (when the first tie in Test history was played out at the Gabba) gave cricket a kiss of life when many were acknowledging it was on its last legs.

TEST RECORD

Batting

Opponents	Debut	M	Inn	N.O	Runs	H.S	50	100	Avrge
England	1953	27	41	2	767	97	4	–	19.67
India	1956/57	8	12	2	144	25			14.40
Pakistan	1956/57	4	6	1	144	56	1	–	28.80
South Africa	1952/53	13	21	2	684	122	1	2	36.00
West Indies	1951/52	11	17	–	462	121	3	1	27.18
Total		63	97	7	2201	122	9	3	24.46

Bowling

Opponents	Debut	M	Ball	Mdns	Runs	Wkts	Avrge	5	Best	Stk/Rt	RPO	Eco/Rt
England	1953	27	7284	289	2641	83	31.82	4	6/70	87.76	2.18	36.26
India	1956/57	8	2953	198	956	52	18.38	5	7/72	56.79	1.94	32.37
Pakistan	1956/57	4	1446	99	416	19	21.89	1	5/93	76.11	1.73	28.77
South Africa	1952/53	13	4136	116	1413	52	27.17	5	5/49	79.54	2.05	34.16
West Indies	1951/52	11	3289	103	1278	42	30.43	1	5/96	78.31	2.33	38.86
Total		63	19108	805	6704	248	27.03	16	7/72	77.05	2.11	35.08

THE GAME IS NOT THE SAME

by Richie Benaud

No game in the past 50 years has changed more than cricket and most of those changes have occurred in the 16 years from 1977. Up to that time a domestic season in Australia consisted of an overseas team beginning its tour in, say, Perth and working around with four-day matches against the States until they then started the first of their five Tests.

Some limited-overs cricket was played, but not a great deal, and the players, other than in England, were very strictly amateur from the monetary point of view, though very professional in their skills.

The year 1977 was the start of a completely different format of the game and of administration. The latter aspect

Richie Benaud scored 121 in 96 minutes (century in 78 minutes) batting at No. 8 in the Fifth Test against the West Indies, Kingston 1955. Australia made 8/758 declared, unique in that Benaud's was one of five centuries—McDonald 127, Harvey 204, Miller 109, Ron Archer 128. In all the West Indies bowled 245.2 overs.

of cricket has always been amateur from the payment point of view although the professional skills may have improved in the past 16 years.

It is a complex game, and often changes to the laws of the game and the playing conditions for a particular tour are engineered by people who have little appreciation of what goes on in the centre of a ground in the heat of a Test match.

The finest example of this came in 1947 when, in England, the administration decided the fast bowlers should be given more of a chance. To accomplish this they introduced a law saying that a new ball could be taken every 55 six-ball overs in first-class cricket. That meant every 40 overs in Australia where there were eight-ball overs.

I imagine Sir Donald Bradman could hardly believe what he read when he and his fellow selectors, Jack Ryder and Chappie Dwyer, sat down to choose the side to tour England in 1948. The games were on uncovered pitches in those days and England's pace bowling attack consisted of Alec Bedser, a great bowler, Bill Edrich, whose career figures were 41 wickets at 41 apiece, Charlie Barnett, Alex Coxon, Dick Pollard, Ken Cranston and Alan Watkins, all medium pacers.

Australia had Ray Lindwall, Keith Miller, Bill Johnston, Ernie Toshack and Sam Loxton.

When I made my debut for New South Wales the following summer, I was batting at No. 3 for my club, Central Cumberland, and gained selection because I scored 160 against Gordon. In the NSW team I was able to bowl overs number 38 and 40 before the second new ball was taken by Lindwall, Miller, Alan Walker, Alan Davidson and Tom Brooks.

It was a crazy law change and it was repealed quickly enough once it was realised that the administrators hadn't thought it through.

This trait, unfortunately, is something that seems to be part of cricket administration and it surfaced again late in the 1950s when administrators over-reacted to some pace bowlers who had an excessive 'drag' in delivery stride.

The result was the front-foot law which has produced more delays in play and wasted time than anything else I can recall.

They have also produced a law relating to short-pitched bowling which, to some, seems a valuable addition to the many strictures on bowlers. Sadly, it has been yet another aspect of taking away the authority of the umpire and the opportunity for him to use his judgment in a game where judgment has always been of vital importance.

In addition, there have been variations in judging what is a 'bouncer', and the one in favour at the moment is where the ball would have passed above the shoulder of the batsman when he is standing upright at the crease. The umpire at square leg must choose a moment when each batsman is standing upright at the crease, which in itself is not easy, then pick out a mark on the far side of the ground which is level with the batsman's shoulder.

Then, any ball passing a few centimetres above that point will be called a no-ball. A ball passing a few centimetres below the base of that letter Q on the advertising hoarding 110 metres away will be legitimate and … I can't go on. It's all too depressing!

One of the best changes to the laws in recent times is the one relating to appeals against the light. The first change came in England where they introduced the words "risk of serious physical injury to the batsman" in the instructions to the umpires for the *only* times they will grant an appeal against the light.

In theory, this is great because it cuts out the chance of umpires, under pressure from batsmen who want to go off, allowing themselves to be talked into saying 'yes'. In practice, we have seen umpires walk off the field when spinners are operating.

No wonder spectators paying a not inconsiderable amount of money at the turnstiles are sometimes very disgruntled at the deal they get. Ninety overs in a day, time wasted through the front-foot law and cricketers walking off when spinners are bowling; it's a wonder the game flourishes as it does in these days of severe competition from all other sports for a share of the spectator's dollar.

One of the saddest changes relates to the umpires themselves where, in recent years, there has been the urging that 'neutral' umpires should be appointed for Test matches. It seems to me a typical piece of administration, in that the root cause of the problem is not that umpires in various countries favour their own side, but that the general standard of umpiring outside England is not all it should be.

When the World Cup was held in Australasia in 1991–92, there were what you might loosely call 'neutral umpires'. There were also just as many mistakes made by those same umpires as would have been the case had they been umpiring with a team from their own country taking part.

Then we had the ultimate in stupid administration. The best umpire, without doubt, in the World Cup was David Shepherd, the roly-poly ex-Gloucestershire batsman, an Englishman.

When England made it to the World Cup Final at the MCG, Shepherd was not allowed to umpire, nor was the Pakistan umpire permitted to stand. There is something wrong, even slightly crazy, with a system which on the one hand wants a certain type of umpire, but then debars the best man!

Now the 'in thing' is to have the third umpire in the room in the pavilion looking at television replays of run-outs. Red and green lights flash, the game is held up (bear in mind you could have four close run-outs in a quarter of an hour), portable telephones beep and cheep and, finally, a decision is made.

I believe it will make the umpires lazy. They will know that for anything within 30 centimetres of being in/out, they *must* call for the third umpire to adjudicate. They will have no need to concentrate as they do now because there will be at least four cameras giving different angles of replays.

The cost of this in an Australian summer? Between $230,000 and $250,000 if it is done properly. Is there some reason why you would not do it properly?

I think there are times when the administrative world of cricket is bonkers. In Australia there will be 30 days of Test cricket and 15 days of limited-overs Internationals. Four extra cameras, four extra tape machines, four extra tape operators, an extra production van. A quarter of a million dollars.

The ACB will have to find that money which, instead, could have been used to improve the standard of umpiring, or been put back into junior cricket for the good of the game!

In England in the past northern summer, a white ball has been used in the Sunday League matches. Not everyone was happy with that, nor with coloured clothing, but it looks as though the experiment will continue. Everyone to whom I spoke was astonished at how much easier it is to see the white ball, although many of the traditionalists stuck to the theme 'If God had wanted us to use white cricket balls He wouldn't have made them red!'

This tends to ignore the fact that all cricket balls are actually white when they are made. They are then dyed red. No one knows why but, presumably, even in the early days of top hats and underarm bowling and coloured shirts, a red ball seemed more suitable.

Cricket terminology may even have had a hand in it. After all, it wouldn't sound quite the same for a commentator to say, "Eighty-five overs have been bowled and Allan Border, if he wishes, now may take the white cherry."

One thing administrators will have to do though is perfect

WHAT'S THE USE TRYING TO POLISH A WHITE BALL ON <u>WHITE</u> TROUSERS...!

the manufacture of the white ball. Because there is no great demand for white balls, which are only used in a handful of night and day games, and there is enormous demand for red balls which are used in all other cricket, no one has cared very much if the white ball is good or indifferent.

But, with suggestions that Test matches and Sheffield Shield matches could be played at night, there will be far more pressure on administrators to get it right.

One of the most disappointing aspects of this has been that over the past 10 years, limited-overs Internationals have produced enormous crowds each playing day. Australia's administrators should have been talking with people like NASA to see what they use for paint and dyes in the nose cones of aeroplanes and space craft, and other areas where there is a need for something to remain bright and shiny white, even taking into account the abrasive nature of the pitch.

You can't talk about playing first-class cricket with two balls, as is done with the limited-overs Internationals in Australia. Administrators, at the moment, are merely being very lazy!

A real test for Australia's administrators will come in the late 1990s when they will have to address the matters of sponsors' dollars, television and marketing of the game. The traditionalists are horrified that the game should be marketed at all, testy that it should *need* to be marketed.

It wasn't done in their day, why should it happen as we approach the 21st century? Channel Nine has set the standard in sports television, not only for other networks in Australia but throughout the world.

The original combination of Kerry Packer and the Head of Sport, David Hill, set out to provide the best ever pictorial coverage of cricket, and succeeded. I don't have access to television in America, other than what I see when covering the Masters Golf each year, but nothing I have seen there, or in any other country, leads me to think that Nine's technical expertise will be overtaken in the near future.

The ACB, by closely observing PBL, has seen what can be done with marketing in sport and they will be keen to show what ability they have. It will be interesting to watch because some think it's just a matter of taking over something and it will automatically work! There is an enormous amount of toil and expertise and common sense to go into it as well.

All this will be tied in with the fact that Benson and Hedges, who have done so much for cricket in Australia, will no longer be able to do that job. The ACB might well be faced with the task of finding four new sponsors and it will be a challenging time for all concerned.

There has never been a time in Australia when more people have been employed by the Australian Cricket Board and the various State associations. Much of the emphasis is on junior cricket, which is good, and both directly and indirectly leads to Under–17 and Under–19 cricket where Australia has been finding young players who have then been able to move into the senior squads.

I hope the various treasurers have been keeping an eye on potential income and escalating expenses, because cricket is only going to become more expensive. There is a limit to what the spectator can and will pay at the gate and it is inconceivable to me that income will stay as it was when Benson and Hedges were the main sponsors.

Tough times ahead, that's why I say it's going to be a very challenging time for our administrators, particularly if television and marketing are separated and the ACB suddenly is paying a great deal of money for things they once received for nothing.

> *Richie Benaud's father Lou, a schoolteacher, once took all 20 wickets in a match, playing for Penrith Waratah Club against St Mary's in Sydney's western suburbs. His 10/30 in the first innings included a haul of four wickets in four balls. In the second innings he took 10/35.*

Chapter Two

Ian Chappell

Born 1943, Ian Michael Chappell, the grandson of Victor Richardson, a courageous, forceful right-hand batsman for Australia in the thirties and an enterprising, unorthodox captain. Ian Chappell had a fair bit of that in his cricket, too!

He was a fierce competitor who never took a backward step, either to a fast bowler or an administrator, and a captain who sought and received fierce loyalty from his players. As a leader he is ranked beside Sir Donald Bradman and Richie Benaud as Australia's finest.

The beginning of his career bears an uncanny resemblance to Benaud's. He too played his first Sheffield Shield match at 18 years of age, and he was 21 on his Test debut. As with Benaud's it was less than memorable.

Against Pakistan, in a one-off Test at the MCG, he batted at No. 3—the position he was later to stamp as his own—and was caught by the wicketkeeper off a right-arm fast-medium bowler named Farooq Hamid. It was to be Farooq's only Test, and Ian Chappell was his one and only Test wicket. Chappell made 11 runs.

Two seasons passed before he played another Test, and then his selection had a twist to it—he was brought in for the final two Tests against Mike Smith's Englishmen as a leg-spinning allrounder who batted at No. 7.

Chappell hit his maiden Test century, 151, against India in the New Year Test at the MCG in 1968. Later in that year he toured England, with Bill Lawry as the Australian captain, where he had only moderate success in the five Tests.

But the selectors' determination to 'blood' him paid off in a big way in the next series. The West Indies, captained by Garfield Sobers, came to Australia for a five-Test series, and Chappell, positioned at his preferred No. 3 in the batting order by Lawry, scored the proverbial 'poultice of runs'.

He hit 548 runs at an average of 68.50, including 117, 165, and 96, yet his success was overshadowed by the remarkable efforts of the man he says he'd always want next to him in a cricket match—Doug Walters.

Walters came back from a cricket-less stint in National Service to record this sequence of scores in that series: 76, 118, 110, 50, 242, 103. So Walters became only the second Australian to score six consecutive Test fifties, the first to score four hundreds in a rubber against the West Indies, and the first batsman ever to score a double-century and a century in the same Test.

Coincidentally, in 1973–74 in New Zealand Ian Chappell's brother Greg became the fourth batsman to achieve the last mentioned feat, a milestone reached in the same innings that Ian himself scored a century in each innings. In so doing they became the first brothers to score hundreds in both innings of a Test match.

Chappell the cricketer will be fondly remembered as a compulsive hooker, who when reminded by critics that the shot was often his downfall instantly reminded his detractors that "it also brings me a helluva lot of runs".

He will be remembered for his crouching, knock-kneed, cupped-hands stance at first slip, where he took 105 catches in Tests.

But ask his fellow players what they think and they'll surely tell you he was the leader who inspired in them the belief that it was always possible to win.

"Things are looking a bit grim" only got a mention in the Chappell phrasebook if he happened to be referring to the state of Australia's opponents.

TEST RECORD

Batting

Opponents	Debut	M	Inn	N.O	Runs	H.S	50	100	Avrge
England	1965/66	31	56	4	2138	192	16	4	41.12
India	1967/68	9	15	1	536	151	1	2	38.29
New Zealand	1973/74	6	10	–	486	145	1	2	48.60
Pakistan	1964/65	4	6	–	352	196	1	1	58.67
South Africa	1966/67	9	18	1	288	49	–	–	16.94
West Indies	1968/69	17	31	4	1545	165	7	5	57.22
Total		76	136	10	5345	196	26	14	42.42

Bowling

Opponents	Debut	M	Ball	Mdns	Runs	Wkts	Avrge	5	Best	Stk/Rt	RPO	Eco/Rt
England	1965/66	31	1022	36	429	6	71.50	–	1/10	170.33	2.52	41.98
India	1967/68	9	370	6	199	1	199.00	–	1/55	370.00	3.23	53.78
New Zealand	1973/74	6	72	–	21	2	10.50	–	1/4	36.00	1.75	29.17
Pakistan	1964/65	4	280	5	117	–	–	–	–	–	2.51	41.79
South Africa	1966/67	9	535	26	296	5	59.20	–	2/91	107.00	3.32	55.33
West Indies	1968/69	17	594	14	254	6	42.33	–	2/21	99.00	2.57	42.76
Total		76	2873	87	1316	20	65.80	–	2/21	143.65	2.75	45.81

Ian Chappell's highest score in Tests was 196 against Pakistan in Adelaide in 1972–73. It came off only 243 balls and included 21 fours and four sixes.

MY TEAM FOR THE TRENCHES

by Ian Chappell

Players: Keith Stackpole   Rod Marsh

Bruce Laird   Graeme Watson

Ian Chappell   Dennis Lillee

Greg Chappell   Ashley Mallett

Ian Redpath   Jeff Thomson

Doug Walters

Managers: Ray Steele, Bill Jacobs

Keith Stackpole always took the attack to the opposition fast bowlers and actually enjoyed them bowling short. He was a fine hooker and cutter, and made such a mess of West Indies pace bowler Uton Dowe at Sabina Park that a wag in the crowd yelled out to the West Indian captain, "Kanhai, you not heard de eleventh commandment? Dowe shall not bowl."

'Stacky' was a thoughtful vice-captain as well as an inspiration to his teammates. I'll never forget Stacky at Queen's Park Oval, Trinidad, in 1973.

He was hit just below the eye while fielding in close and when he was helped from the ground he wanted to fight a small section of the crowd who cheered. A few hours later he came lumbering out onto the ground with his head bandaged to congratulate us on winning a close-fought Test match.

Bruce Laird was a fine player of fast bowling. He had bundles of courage, was a good cutter and an excellent team player. He took so many pummellings from the fast bowlers without flinching or complaining that he was known as

> *In the 1973–74 season in the Sheffield Shield Ian and Greg Chappell freakishly scored the same number of runs at an identical average in matches against Victoria, Greg with Queensland and Ian with South Australia. The aggregate was 449 runs, the average 149.66!*

'Bruised' Laird, although his real nickname was 'Stumpy'.

He made a magnificent century in World Series Cricket at Port-of-Spain, Trinidad, after we'd slumped to 5/22. Australia went on to win the game by 20-odd runs. After that knock, West Indies opener Roy Fredericks paid him a great tribute when he said, "Stumpy I wish I'd played that innings."

Ian Chappell I was asked for the 10 guys I'd most like at my side when the going is tough. I don't believe in the position of coach, so I've assumed I'm captain. In that case my preference is to bat at No. 3.

Greg Chappell was a magnificent player of pace bowling and no one was more determined when aroused. I discovered that in the backyard when he was about nine. I believed Greg to be out caught behind off my bowling but he wouldn't admit he'd hit the ball. He still denied it even when I had his arm twisted up his back, and then when he safely negotiated a barrage of bouncers I knew I had a battle on my hands.

Greg always said, "Test cricket was a breeze after playing backyard matches against Ian."

Ian Redpath made three hundreds in 1975–76 as an opener against the West Indian pair Andy Roberts and Michael Holding. He wasn't the most elegant player of fast bowling but he was effective.

No one sold his wicket more dearly than 'Redda'. After battling for ages on a damp Adelaide Oval pitch against

'Deadly' Derek Underwood, Redda was given out in doubtful circumstances. He sat dejected in the dressingroom for a couple of minutes without taking off his pads, then picked up his bat and spat on it.

Doug Walters The word guts has a few different connotations. No one had more mental strength than 'Dashing Doug' when it came to counter-attacking if his team was in trouble. And no Australian player of my time was more successful playing in that manner.

I can think of two Tests, Auckland in 1973–74 and Adelaide 1974–75 when he came in on wet pitches with Australia in trouble and his counter-attack not only got us out of trouble, but eventually helped us to win.

There were some mornings when he showed a lot of guts just turning up, never mind actually performing on the field.

Despite his penchant for late nights, I can only remember him being off the field once. He'd had a longer night than John Hewson had on March 13, 1993, when I brought him on to bowl against New Zealand at the Sydney Cricket Ground. When he limped off the ground with a sprained ankle, injured while appealing for lbw, he had figures of 3/9, as the Kiwis collapsed from 0/78 to 3/90. His third victim was Bev Congdon, the man he'd been appealing against when he sprained his ankle.

Rod Marsh played in 96 Tests for Australia and never missed one through injury. In fact he would have kept to every ball bowled if the captain hadn't been so stupid as to let him bowl 10 overs against Pakistan in a drawn game.

'Bacchus' managed this feat of human endurance, despite being twice hit flush on the forearms by Dennis Lillee at Trent Bridge in 1972, when accidental full tosses bounced just in front of him. I'll never understand how they didn't shatter his arm.

He also withstood the brunt of Jeff Thomson's thunderbolts when he was frighteningly fast. As one such thunderbolt smashed into his glove way above his head, Rodney exclaimed, "Christ that hurts. But I love it."

However, Rod did have one advantage when it came to endurance—two legs that are stronger than the Empire State Building's foundations.

Graeme 'Beatle' Watson was an allrounder who had more guts than he had sense at times. He played virtually the full

1971–72 season for Western Australia with a broken bone in his leg. That season he bowled the fastest of his career and Marsh said that at times he was as quick as Lillee.

He was also hit in the nose at the MCG when a ball accidentally slipped out of Tony Greig's fingers in an International against the Rest Of The World. Unfortunately Graeme haemorrhaged in hospital a few days later and his heart actually stopped beating on two occasions. Three weeks after being discharged from hospital he was playing for WA, when South Australia opening bowler Kevin McCarthy hit Graeme in the back of his head as he missed a hook shot. He batted on and a couple of weeks later was selected for the England tour of 1972.

> *In the 1976–77 Gillette Cup (forerunner to the Mercantile Mutual Cup) in Perth Queensland dismissed Western Australia for 77. Dennis Lillee got Viv Richards for a 'duck' and Greg Chappell for nine in Queensland's reply of 62.*

Dennis Lillee was a captain's dream and a batsman's nightmare. On a few occasions it was said I over-bowled Lillee. Have you ever considered taking a bone from a Doberman?

No? Well, that's why I didn't take the ball from Dennis Lillee.

Dennis actually says I was responsible for his first back injury. Bowling against Pakistan at the SCG in 1972–73 he delivered a leg break. At the end of the over I said, "I already have three leg-spinners in the side, if I want any bowled I'll call on one of them."

Dennis says he tried to bowl so "bloody fast" in his next over he hurt his back.

In that match he climbed off the massage table when we were eight second innings wickets down and only 80-odd in front and declared, "I'm going to bowl in the second innings."

I replied, "Don't be bloody stupid—we couldn't win this if we had four Dennis Lillees bowling."

However, Bob Massie and John Watkins put on 83 runs for the ninth wicket and we finished with a lead of 158. "I'm definitely going to bowl now," Dennis said.

And bowl he did, for 23 overs on the trot. He only took two wickets, but the sight of Lillee walking through the gate gave us a great psychological advantage. He then broke a stump when he bowled opener Nasim-ul-Ghani and I reckon that was worth four wickets on its own.

Ashley Mallett 'Rowdy' was a fine off-spinner with a big heart. As well as taking wickets he could take his punishment. He didn't like it and it made him quietly angry, but it also made him bowl better.

Playing for Queensland, brother Greg tried to hit Ashley out of the attack and took 18 off the over. Mallett's next three overs were probably the best I ever saw him bowl. They were maidens and Greg was hard pushed to stay in, never mind score.

As a batsman Mallett could be stubborn, as in hard to get out and like a donkey.

He had his finger broken by a Lillee bouncer in Perth in a tight Shield game. I told Ashley he was to bat at No. 11 in the second innings and then only in an emergency. We still required a handful of runs for victory when the eighth wicket fell (to Lillee) and Mallett pushed past Wayne Prior who was padded up and marched to the crease.

When he fended off the first ball, SA's wicketkeeper Mike 'Jimmy' Hendricks was almost standing next to him so that Mallett couldn't get down the non-striker's end. Not satisfied, Mallett ran a single off the next ball and finally cut Lillee off the end of the bat and ran the winning runs holding his hand against his body to dull the pain.

When he came back to the dressingroom he couldn't stop his hand from shaking and he looked like a man in the final stages of Parkinson's disease. I went over to him and said, "Thanks Rowd, but you're a bloody idiot." I couldn't say anymore, I was on the verge of tears.

Jeff Thomson For two and half years (before he busted his shoulder) 'Two Up' was the most lethal bowler I've seen. That means you pick him in your side so he doesn't finish up playing against you.

Jeff had the guts to remain true to himself. He was a fast bowler and he was prepared to live or die on speed. In 1979 in the SuperTest at Queen's Park Oval, he took five wickets in the first innings. In the second on a dry dusty, low-bouncing pitch he was virtually un-bowlable apart from a short spell with the new ball.

We finished up winning the game by just over 20 runs as Lillee, Pascoe and a bit of spin dismissed the West Indies. Over a celebratory beer, I dragged 'Thommo' aside and suggested he have a chat to Dennis about bowling on slow pitches.

Thommo said, "I know what you're saying mate, but if you don't mind I'd like to do it my way."

That's when I realised that Thommo loved being a fast bowler and he wasn't going to compromise for anybody.

The most knowledgeable cricket fans in the world are found at Kensington Oval, Barbados. Now bear in mind that they regularly watch the West Indies pace bowlers in action, with the likes of Herman Griffith, Manny Martindale (genuine quicks from around the 1930s), Wes Hall, Charlie Griffith, Malcolm Marshall and Joel Garner, who also played for Barbados. They know what genuine pace looks like.

In 1978–79 they witnessed Jeffrey Robert Thomson take on a renowned good player of pace in Isaac Vivian Alexander Richards. When we toured the Caribbean 12 months later they were still talking about Thommo's pace in that spell. When I went back to Barbados in 1991 I asked, "What is the fastest bowling you guys have seen?"

The chorused answer to my question was, "Oooh, Thomson maan. Thommo to Richards, dat de quickes' bowlin'."

Manager: If the tour was England, *Ray Steele*. The Caribbean, *Bill Jacobs*.

Both men are Victorians and disciplinarians. But they also know how to enjoy themselves when the time is right.

In England in 1972 I missed the plane to Scotland (I wasn't playing in the match) and finished up in London playing golf with Rod Marsh. We were thirsty after golf and at three a.m. we were drinking cold Foster's at Richie Benaud's flat, when I realised that the manager didn't know where I was.

So I rang Ray in Scotland. A gruff voice said, " 'Ello." And I replied, "Is that the manager of the Australian cricket team?"

" 'Corse 'tis," came the terse reply.

"Well this is the Australian captain," I said, "just ringing to let you know I missed the plane."

The next night I was sleeping soundly at the Waldorf in London when the phone rang. "Is that the Australian captain?" came a voice at the other end.

" 'Corse 'tis," was my sleepy reply.

"Well this is the Australian manager," chortled Ray, "just calling to let you know it's four a.m."

When we were thrashed by England in the Fourth Test at Headingley, there was some doubt about the pitch preparation. The groundsman said it had been infected by a fungus, Fuserium.

Ray Steele said, "I don't want to hear one word of complaint from anyone in the Australian team." No one from the touring party whinged and we got on with the job of levelling the series by winning the Fifth Test. Ray Steele contributed to that victory.

My first tour was to South Africa in 1966–67. Along with my roommate Graeme Watson, and Brian Taber and Dave Renneberg, I was delayed a little in getting to an official function at the Australian High Commissioner's house in Johannesburg.

When I say delayed a little, the function started at 7.30 p.m. and we arrived about, oh say 3 or 4 uhmm, well er, hours rather than minutes late. By that time the rest of the touring party, except for manager Bill 'Fagin' Jacobs, had left the function.

Fagin strode across to our car, ignored our muttered

Good evenings and simply said, "You bastards are in trouble. Be in my room at nine o'clock tomorrow morning."

We were in Fagin's room before nine and he told us exactly what he thought of us. He said that in future he expected us to arrive five minutes before the rest of the team and if any of us were late again we'd be sent home.

The next morning I headed the foursome as we walked down the stairs to the foyer. Bill was standing near the door, so I thought to myself, "Let's see if this guy has a sense of humour."

"Privates Watson, Taber, Renneberg and Chappell, reporting saar," I said in a firm voice as I essayed a salute and clicked my heels together.

Without a smile Bill returned the salute and said, "All present and accounted forrr. At ease private."

Bill and I have remained friends ever since, but I must add that I've never been late for any appointment where he's involved.

Come to think of it, Fagin did such a good job negotiating meal allowances for the team in the Caribbean on the 1973 tour, let's make him the treasurer and Ray the manager.

Chapter Three

David Gower

Born 1957, David Ivon Gower, later to become one of the world's classiest batsmen. He is a left-hander, a trait he shares on the commentary team with Australia's Bill Lawry. Gower has the most Test runs but Lawry has the average.

Another thing they have in common is they were both sacked as their country's captain. If Gower is bitter over that, or over any of the other strange selection policies sometimes applied to him, then he keeps it well camouflaged behind that apparently unflappable exterior.

'Laid back' is the term most often applied to his cricketing attitude, and it was clearly in evidence on his Test debut against Pakistan at the Oval in 1978. From the second ball he received from Liaquat Ali he hooked a four, his first scoring shot in Test cricket.

Fourteen seasons later he hit Pakistan's Aaqib Javed for four at Old Trafford, to reach a career Test aggregate of 8114 and surpass Geoffrey Boycott as England's leading run-getter. He is currently at 8231 but any advance on that appears dependent on the whims of the England selection panel.

When Gower arrived on the English County scene with

Leicestershire in 1975, many of the game's followers drew an instant comparison with the great Frank Woolley. H S Altham, the greatest of all cricket historians, once described Woolley as "a tall and graceful figure, who with his quiet air and unhurried movements, brought to his left-handed batting an unmistakable air of majestic almost casual command".

And so did Gower play until in recent times his critics have seized upon those very attributes and demanded he become more orthodox in his ways, more conformist in matters of training and practice.

Another cricketing 'non-conformist' was Australia's Doug Walters, who once told a team trainer who demanded he run up and down a hill a seemingly risky number of times, that he didn't think such exercise would help him much against a leg-spinning delivery pitched on leg and designed to hit off.

Like Walters Gower has an impressive record to back the 'I'll do it my way' theory. His 18 Test centuries place him 16th on the all-time list of "most centuries". He went 119 Test innings without registering a 'duck'—a record.

Until he suffered major throwing shoulder damage he was an outstanding fieldsman in the 'run-out' positions—short cover and short mid-wicket.

Gower had a unique talent that brought him, and England, much success; but more than that he brought joy to tens of thousands of cricket fans around the world.

David Gower was the quickest player to 100 Tests —10 years and 50 days, about four years faster than the previous quickest. It underlined the dramatic increase in the amount of Test cricket being played in modern times.

TEST RECORD

Batting

Opponents	Debut	M	Inn	N.O	Runs	H.S	50	100	Avrge
Australia	1978/79	42	77	4	3269	215	12	9	´44.78
India	1979	24	37	6	1391	*200	6	2	44.87
New Zealand	1978	13	22	1	1051	131	4	4	50.05
Pakistan	1978	17	27	3	1185	*173	9	2	49.38
Sri Lanka	1981/82	2	3	1	186	89	2	–	93.00
West Indies	1980	19	38	3	1149	*154	6	1	32.83
Total		117	204	18	8231	215	39	18	44.25

* denotes not out

OF CRICKET'S RICH TAPESTRY ...

by David Gower

Anyone who has ever played the game of cricket to something approaching the highest level will immediately attest to the immense satisfaction of playing the game well.

For a committed Englishman like myself, the ultimate cricketing dream involves leading England to glorious victory over Australia in an Ashes series, both as captain and leading run-scorer, with the chance to hold aloft the cherished urn at the end of it all in front of an appreciative capacity crowd.

Fortunately for me I can at least say that I did once achieve that dream, even up to that final detail, when England won the 1985 series by clinching the final Test at the Oval to make it a three–one winning margin.

Admittedly it was not quite a full house on a Monday afternoon in London, but those that were there seemed to have enjoyed themselves. And admittedly, when Peter West, the BBC's presenter on the day, presented me publicly with a replica of the Ashes—I thought at the time as a permanent memento—another little man from the 'Beeb' took it back off me 30 seconds later, explaining that even if it was a replica the museum at Lord's still wanted it back!

It would be churlish of me to turn this into a full-scale whinge, as the satisfaction of that summer's success will live on in my mind forever, especially when I consider all the Ashes series in which I have been involved, and the varying degrees of success and failure—the 'twin impostors'—that have come with it.

For instance, if 1985 was a pinnacle for me both as a captain and a batsman—and it remains the most successful series of my career by some distance—then 'Border's revenge' four years later is in the record books as the stern reminder that you can't always write your own scripts. Come to think of it, the man who has come closest to achieving that sort of control is one Ian Botham, one who really did make his mark in no uncertain terms on a number of Ashes contests. But even he has had to bow to the whims of selectors and the unpredictability of his own form and fitness over the years.

Ironically, there were a number of similarities between those two series, even if the results were just about diametrically opposite, with Australia's winning margin in 1989 being even greater than England's when my dreams were coming true.

There were the standard quotes at the start of each series about how even a contest we could all expect over the summer; while, with all due respect paid to the opposition in public, our private team meetings emphasised merely how we were going to "beat the XXXX" out of our visitors. Of course, that was fine in '85, but it involved somewhat more humble pie by September '89!

Also, both series were affected by rebel tours to South Africa, first with AB's '85 touring party incorporating players who had weeks previously been bound for a completely different continent, until re-negotiation put them back on a Qantas flight direct to London. How much it created an atmosphere that ruined their chances of success is debatable. I tend to think that an Ashes side unites against the enemy whatever problems come their way, and fights in spite of any such distractions.

Indeed that series was still quite even at one–all going into the last two games of the series, and the breakthrough, as far as we were concerned, came only when Wayne Phillips' attempt to pierce the cover field at Edgbaston got no further than Allan Lamb's instep, and thence popped gently into my hands at silly point.

It was a freak, and I have to say genuine, dismissal, which ended a brave counter-attacking innings and also marked the beginning of the end for the tourists, whose resistance was broken from then on.

It also wiped away the smirk that had brightened AB's face that morning when it looked as though rain would linger on through the day and save him and his side.

But if '85 found Australia wanting, '89 demonstrated the Brits at their most perverse. It started with the sort of confusion that never bodes well for the immediate future, when the selectors chose Mike Gatting as their captain for the summer, only to have him vetoed by one of Lord's well-hidden mandarins, a fellow by the name of Ossie Wheatley. I suppose we should rename him 'Aussie' for his efforts, although I suspect he is not universally known in Australia, having been a long-serving County cricketer for Glamorgan before moving to responsibility at HQ.

Anyway it was his intervention that forced the selectors to offer me the job instead, even though I had no idea of the background to the offer. As I had been keen to take up the reins again in any case, I cannot really complain too much about the route to office, only about the way the series developed.

At the start I was genuinely optimistic about our chances of another '85-type summer, but I obviously failed to spot the change in AB's attitude to Test captaincy, which now appeared to put success before anything else, especially public charm, and which was completely vindicated by the end of the summer. It was over a bottle or two of Bollinger in my back garden late in the summer, when the series was all but decided, that AB finally started to relax, almost but not quite apologising for his demeanour in the past few months, and understandably delighted that his leadership had brought about such a reversal of fortunes.

What I had also failed to spot, or had hidden from me, or both, was that this time it was England's turn to be undermined by the rebels, though once again I would not overplay the significance. In truth we were outplayed by the Australians, and we were hampered more by injuries than defections. However, I was not overjoyed to be the last to hear of the planned tour that my competitor for the captaincy was due to lead to South Africa in the autumn, news that broke publically at Manchester during the Test that was to confirm Australia's recapturing of the Ashes.

The comparisons that these two series evoke are almost a cautionary tale for professional cricketers, highlighting the ups and downs of their existence, and reminding me how thin the line is that separates victory from defeat and success from failure.

But more than that these trials and tribulations also teach you to view cricket and life in some sort of acceptable perspective, to suffer your disappointments but then put them behind you pretty damn quick so that you move on to the next challenge with renewed optimism. The alternative is merely to sit and mope, cursing your ill fortune, until your friends get suitably pissed off with you and rightly leave you to sort yourself out or do the decent thing and pull the trigger before you make everyone else miserable too. In other words, yes, it is up to a point only a game of cricket, and best you make sure you win the next one.

True, when considering matters of national importance such as Ashes series, we are talking important games of cricket, and we cannot be seen to be taking things lightly.

In my autobiography, imaginatively called *Gower, the Autobiography* to avoid confusion (damned clever these publisher chappies when it comes to book titles), I did try to refute allegations about the 'laid back' way of life that is portrayed as my chosen existence.

But actually there is definitely something to be said for cultivating that sort of attitude, especially if it helps you cope with the deep shame that comes with having the XXXX beaten out of you on a cricket field by a horde of marauding Australians, when the whole nation, England that is, is

hoping for something rather different.

The first problem comes when people perceive you as indifferent when things go wrong, as opposed to being able to cope manfully with the disappointment by trying to shrug it all off.

The second problem comes when people like selectors and captains then begin to question your 'commitment' or 'attitude'.

Naturally, although this may sound like it could apply to anyone, I have the odd axe to grind on this topic, and once again one can draw comparisons between England and Australia, as both countries' cricket is now being run by people with remarkably similar theories.

In short we are seeing the 'work ethic' in operation with both squads: the only route to the right results is the one which involves rigorous training and practice schedules and the dogma that hard work alone will bring success.

I don't profess to know the ins and outs of Bob Simpson's routines apart from what I have seen from the other side of the SCG and other venues, but I have had closer exposure to the way England have operated under Graham Gooch, Micky Stewart, and now Keith Fletcher.

Now I certainly do not argue with the fact that all athletes must prepare properly for their sports, and in particular for the big event, in cricket's case the Test match or one-day International.

Where I beg to differ from much current thinking is my belief in the benefits of relaxation away from the game that dominates our lives as professional cricketers.

To me it is painfully obvious, normally round about the third lap of the oval or the middle of the afternoon when practice seems to be intruding somewhat late into the day, that individuals need to be treated in a variety of ways. Surely the skill of a good captain is in blending the many different characters at his disposal into a cohesive and effective unit; to just treat them all as one amorphous mass is far too simple an approach. One for all and all for one was best left to the three musketeers of fiction, and does not translate so well from the original French into cricketing reality.

If I may drag my mate Mr Botham back as a witness—he is as convinced as I am of the need for outside interests to keep the mind fresh for cricket—Ian is adamant that England lost the last World Cup not so much on the MCG against Pakistan, although Pakistan did play rather well on the night, but more in the practice nets over the last week or two of a very demanding tournament.

Basically, England were knackered, with injuries and weariness just overcoming the importance and adrenalin of the big occasion. Not to mention the odd strange selection, such as leaving out Robin Smith who, as far as I can remember, is rather a good one-day player.

The truth is that what works for some players will not work for all. Geoff Boycott based his game on immaculate and painstaking preparation, as does Graham Gooch. I do not question the validity of their methods, which is amply borne out by their results in Test cricket. It is merely worth looking at the Gowers, the Bothams, the Lambs, who have succeeded with slightly different outlooks.

Character does count, both in the sense that we all possess different ones, and that, however much we all train and practise, what counts is the character and ability of the player on the field of play.

The benefit of having 'characters' around is also immeasurable. For the first time in many years in the winter of 1992–93 England went abroad without any of the three men mentioned in the previous paragraph, and whatever you might think of me, I can assure you that Botham and Lamb rank as true personalities in this game. Just ask anyone who has played with or against them over the years!

Now I am not saying by any stretch of the imagination that that is the reason England lost to India and Sri Lanka, but there is real value in having someone of the stature of Ian Botham in your side. Apart from great natural ability, one of Ian's great assets was his heart and spirit that lifted a team to greater heights, maybe not every day of every week, but enough to make the difference to all of the sides that he has represented.

Nor am I condoning every whim that came to the minds of the three of us now and again, but we should all remember that good humour oils a lot of wheels, even in the context of international cricket. A lot of the stories dare not be told, but simple little things do make the day go by quicker, and how much simpler can you get than asking one of the world's best known if nervy umpires, Dicky Bird, to hang on to your mobile phone when you come out for the post-lunch session, as Lambie did at Lord's, telling Dicky that he was expecting an urgent call.

When the phone predictably rang some minutes later, Dicky, who freely admits that the rules of cricket are more his forte than the miracles of modern technology, just could not cope, to the amusement of all concerned.

I have also done some pretty stupid things in my time, top of the list being to park a hire car on the bottom of the lake in St Moritz, having misjudged the degrees of thick and thin ice available to keep this particular motor car on top of things as opposed to several fathoms below the most effective cruising altitude. That makes it sound a bit as though I also got confused about what sort of transport I was driving at the time, perhaps forgetting that I had no wings available to support me.

Which brings me nicely on to Tiger Moths and the end of my thesis on how to be successful in Test cricket and enjoy yourself at the same time. When I took to the air over Carrara on England's visit there in 1990–91, it was without

much obvious consideration of the ramifications or the likely reaction of our management.

I had watched the Moths regularly take off on sightseeing flights over the Gold Coast from the airstrip that lay so close to the stadium and the temptation was too much.

What many observers of my jaunt failed to appreciate was the precision of the planning that preceded the trip, with regular phone calls back to the stadium, right up until take-off, checking that neither Smith nor Lamb had got out and precipitated the sort of collapse that had been dogging our tour.

Once in the air we knew that from 200 feet (60 metres) above the ground we would see quite clearly whether wickets had been or were falling, so I was confident of not being found missing should we be required to field sooner than otherwise expected.

Where I was adjudged horribly wrong was in thinking that the jaunt could be interpreted as harmless fun, a morale booster on one of the few days that were going well for us on the field during an otherwise pretty desperate tour, and I still see it all in that light, even if the management decided that 20 minutes in the air was worth a cool $2500. I was lucky I hadn't spent all my tour expenses by then!

More of a worry, though, is that my self-expression on that tour might have told against me when the side was picked to go to India in 1992–93, and there was no space left for me by the time the old rebels and young hopefuls had taken their spots. Having come back into the side against Pakistan and done well against Wasim, Waqar and Co, there had to be something else in the minds of the selectors than just the question of how to win the Tests in the subcontinent.

Perhaps one day all will be revealed in an as yet unwritten tome that might escape the TCCB censors some time in the future.

Chapter Four

Bill Lawry

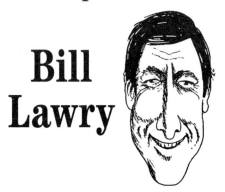

Born 1937, William Morris Lawry, but known throughout the cricket world as 'Bill'. In his early career there was a temptation to tag him with 'Barnacle' as well, so slow was his scoring on occasions after making his debut for Victoria a day before he turned 19.

He toured England in 1961 and at Lord's in the Second Test played one of the game's great knocks. In the face of physical torment from England's fine pace pair, Trueman and Statham, who exploited a ridge in the pitch to land blow after blow to Lawry's body and hands, he scored 130 and set Australia on the way to a five-wicket victory. That Test was also notable in that the Australian captain was Neil Harvey; it was the only time he took the reins for his country.

Lawry scored 2019 runs in all matches on that tour at a high average of 61.18 and with nine centuries, yet he had begun the tour as a relative unknown, a tall, rookie left-hand opening batsman most likely to play second fiddle to the more established Colin McDonald, and Bob Simpson, now Australia's coach.

Simpson was moved down the order, but in the Fourth Test opened with Lawry, thus beginning the partnership that was to become legendary for its massive scoring feats, highlighted by its sharp running between the wickets. Together they figured in nine century opening stands, the grandest of all being 382 put together at Bridgetown, Barbados, on Australia's 1965 tour to the West Indies. Lawry scored 210 and Simpson 201, the first opening pair in Test history to score double-centuries in the same innings.

On his return to Australia from the 1961 Ashes tour Lawry was made captain of Victoria, a clear signal that he was being groomed for the Australian job, which eventually came his way on the retirement of Simpson after the series against India in 1967–68.

He was the 13th Victorian-born Test captain, and that proved to be an unlucky portent. After his team received a mauling from the powerful South African team of the late sixties, followed by lacklustre showings in the early Tests of the 1970–71 Ashes series in Australia, the selectors axed Lawry as captain for the final Test.

Not only that, they dropped him from the team. Ian Chappell, his successor as captain, was later to describe the selectors' decision as "the most insensitive thing I have seen done in more than fifteen years of first-class cricket."

It was a terribly sad end to a great career. Lawry, who was an accomplished player of the hook shot, was at his best against aggressive fast bowling, but struggled against spin. That inevitably slowed his run rate, and inspired wisecracks from barrackers.

He once dawdled for four hours over 45 runs in an Ashes Test. In the midst of this grim defence, a short while after he'd hit a boundary, a barracker pleaded, "Come on 'Lightning', strike again!"

When chided by the critics over his slower offerings Lawry used to say, "Yes, but just imagine how many runs I'll get when I do bat well."

TEST RECORD

Batting

Opponents	Debut	M	Inn	N.O	Runs	H.S	50	100	Avrge
England	1961	30	51	5	2233	166	13	7	48.54
India	1964/65	12	23	4	892	100	7	1	46.95
Pakistan	1964/65	2	4	–	89	41	–	–	22.25
South Africa	1963/64	14	28	1	985	157	4	1	36.48
West Indies	1964/65	10	17	2	1035	210	3	4	69.00
Total		68	123	12	5234	210	27	13	47.15

A TANGLED WEB WE WEAVED

by Bill Lawry

It was 1961, and I'd just got about the best news any young cricketer can get, news that I'd been selected to make the Ashes tour to England. At that stage I hadn't even played a Test match on my own territory.

All my cricket had been with my beloved Victoria, where I had been lucky enough to enter the ranks of first-class cricket under captains such as Sam Loxton, Len Maddocks, Colin McDonald and Neil Harvey.

They were all good, and very positive captains as well as fine cricketers and each in his own way had some influence on my attitude to the game. Those were the days when Sheffield Shield clashes between Victoria and New South

Bill Lawry hit 15 sixes in his Test career, including three against England at Old Trafford, 1968, when he scored 81, and the same number, same place in 1964 when he scored 106.

Wales were classics, in fact as hard-fought as any Test match.

So, even though I had yet to play a Test I felt I had come through a pretty tough school. The captain for the tour to England was Richie Benaud, and his vice-captain Neil Harvey.

I'd watched Richie Benaud lead Australia with great success against England in 1958 when they won the Ashes four–nil in Australia. Then followed the wonderful tour to Australia by the West Indies in 1960–61, when Benaud led the Australians to a nail-biting two–one series win.

At the end of the day everybody conceded that the captains, Benaud and Frank Worrell, had, if not saved Test cricket, certainly given it a great push for the sixties.

Many people thought it was the turning point in the rejuvenation of the positive side of the game. So as a 24-year-old, going on my first tour with two great cricketers Benaud and Harvey as tour leaders promised to be a wonderful experience.

It turned out to be just that, so much so that now, 30 years on, not only do I remain convinced Richie Benaud was the best captain I played under, but we have remained close friends.

These days, one of the highlights of my cricketing year comes during the Sydney Test match when I go out to Richie and Daphne Benaud's place with a few friends for Saturday night dinner, and to talk cricket.

I honestly believe that every time I leave Richie's place I have learnt something more about the great game. There is no doubt in my mind that he has the best cricketing brain in modern cricket—whether he's discussing something happening on the field, or off it.

But in 1961 I barely knew him. I'd played against him, and I'd watched him, but if you don't know, or have never met Richie, then he can seem aloof or distant.

> *Richie Benaud took 5/12 in 25 balls to skittle England in the famous Old Trafford Test of 1961.*

In those days the team travelled to England by boat, or ocean liner, the one we were to sail on being the *Himalaya*. The Cricket Board had decided we should play a couple of practice matches on the way to England, one in Hobart and another at Perth, for two reasons. It was a way of bringing the game to Tasmania, then what might be called the outpost of Australian cricket, a sort of public relations exercise, and we would board the *Himalaya* at Fremantle, south of Perth, from where she was to sail.

For the first few weeks on the boat I sat back a bit. I spent most of the time with Graham McKenzie, who was 19 and the 'baby' of the tour, and Frank Misson, the lanky fast bowler from NSW, who was 22.

One of the tour 'veterans' Ken Mackay, the great Queensland allrounder, was often with us. Mackay, or 'Slasher' as he was known within the team—one of those reverse nicknames, it was a reference to his stodgy batsmanship—virtually took the younger players under his wing on the boat trip over.

Not only that but once we arrived in England it was Ken Mackay who took the time to bowl to the younger batsmen in the nets. And whenever I wasn't selected to play in a game early in the tour, on the days off, everyday, he would come down to Lord's with Frank Misson and me and bowl for hours. It was a turning point for me, because it gave me confidence to handle the strange conditions.

It was many years later that I found out Ken Mackay had agreed with Richie Benaud that he would be the ideal guy to encourage the younger players touring for the first time; Slasher rarely had a drink, he didn't smoke, and above all he was one of the most dedicated cricketers I ever knew.

I had a great run on the tour. I made a century in the Lord's Test, a magic moment for any cricketer, and continued to score hundreds fairly freely, which put me in the position where, with continuing success, I could score 2000 runs on my first tour to England.

It was a milestone I wouldn't have even dared dream about when I boarded the boat in Fremantle. But the pressure told, and after I had spent a long time over a few ordinary runs in a match against The Gentlemen of England XI, Richie Benaud came to me.

He said, "I believe you are stale and you need a spell. I'm going to give you a couple of games off. Get away, go and visit friends, do whatever you want, go to the theatre, go out, but don't pick up a cricket bat for ten or twelve days."

It was just the pick-me-up I needed.

It was a super tour for mateship, too. Because overseas cricket tours were quite lengthy then—in 1961 we were away from March 29 until September 26, being the last team to sail to England, then back again—different groups tended to stick together.

The veterans like the Benauds, the Harveys, the Davidsons, were touring for the third or fourth time and had become great friends, and they forged great friendships with a lot of English people, so they'd often head off together.

The younger ones on their first tour, like me, also tended to go everywhere together, and lasting friendships were struck. I became very good friends with Frank Misson. Frank won't be remembered as one of the all-time great fast bowlers, but certainly I will remember him as one of the best team men you could ever wish for.

Frank was, if not the first then certainly among the first of cricket's fitness fanatics. His eating habits made headlines—lots of muesli, nuts and honey were a staple part of Frank's diet. The other side to his fitness regime was his running.

I remember a Sheffield Shield match before that tour when Victoria played NSW in 44 degree heat and Frank bowled all day, then while the rest of us were showering and changing Frank pulled on a pair of running shorts and did 15 to 20 laps of the MCG.

Frank was always trying to be a better bowler and felt that fitness was important to that end. I guess you could say Frank was before his time, because what he did in the late fifties and early sixties is the norm today for fast bowlers aiming to get fit—they do a lot of roadwork and look after their bodies either in the gym, or by what they eat and drink. Frank was certainly doing all that on our tour to England in 1961.

Frank was a gentleman, a likeable guy with a lot of charm. I thought he wouldn't have looked out of place on that tour had he taken to wearing a bowler hat and carrying a cane.

He had a shock of blond, shortish hair, was tall, and his throaty chuckle and twinkling eyes left no one in any doubt that he had a wonderful sense of humour. He did little things that made everybody laugh.

On that tour when we played Yorkshire we stayed in Harrogate in one of those great old majestic English hotels, all polished wood and massive rooms, proper silver cutlery in the dining room. Anyone who has been to Harrogate will know the one I mean.

One night we arrived at the dining room late, which was not done, but Frank, because of his charm, always had the waitresses fussing around him, no matter whether they were 18, 28 or 58 years old.

This particular night the waitress came over to Frank and asked, "What would you like for tea?" Frank looked up from his menu, wished her good evening with the white flash of a smile, and replied, "I would like plenty of vegetables and I would like my steak well done, thank you. I want carrots, potatoes, broccoli and any other greens you have."

The waitress was writing away on her pad, then stopped and said, "And how do you want them?"

Frank reached out and gently took the pencil from her hand, raised the index of his left hand as if to say "watch this", then took his plate and proceeded, with the pencil, to draw on the plate exactly where he wanted the potatoes, the broccoli and anything else.

And Frank had that waitress, who must have been 58 years of age, hanging about him like a mother for the rest of our stay. That was Frank.

The physiotherapist on that tour was Arthur James, a man who had been on every tour to England since 1930, rubbing shoulders with the Woodfulls, the Bradmans, the Hassetts, the Fleetwood-Smiths, the Millers.

Arthur laughed as hard as any of us that night, and said, "This bloke's got the greatest charm of any man I've ever been away with, and he's only twenty-two years of age and on his first tour!"

Our team manager in 1961 was Syd Webb, a QC, a man small in stature, as square as he was tall.

He loved a whisky did Syd; used to judge a County by the number of whiskies he had with its committeemen before lunch rather than by the condition of the pitch and ground.

Syd was a very likeable guy, but he also had a bit of fire in his belly. That was apparent when he decided Richie Benaud was getting too much press, and so 'gagged' him, which was a very foolish thing to do. Managers who go round 'gagging' captains leave themselves open to some critical press. The gag only lasted about a couple of days.

The thing about Syd was he liked to be noticed, and that just wasn't happening because the high-flying players like Richie Benaud, Neil Harvey and Alan Davidson were most sought after. Frank Misson picked up on Syd's frustration early on in the tour.

One of Frank's pranks was, when we were all sitting down to dinner at our hotel, to hand a little note to the waitress—who of course he had eating out of the palm of his hand—and she would take it out to the reception.

There would be an announcement: "Would the manager of the Australian cricket team, Mr Syd Webb, please report to reception."

Of course, Syd loved to be paged. The dining room in hotels in England is a very big deal—they love their dining rooms—and everyone would stop eating and look at Syd as he pushed back his chair and rushed out.

Then he'd come back, and five minutes later Frank would repeat the prank, and off Syd would go again, but never once did he come back and say, "Nobody there."

Every time Frank went to London he'd always go into the magic shop, where one day he bought what we called 'The Pumper'. This was a device that consisted of a small bladder, attached to which was a small squeeze-pump.

Frank usually waited until Syd had had one or two whiskies before pulling the 'page prank'. When Syd was absent from the dinner table Frank would put the pumper under the tablecloth and under Syd's plate.

Syd returned and we'd all be sitting there waiting for him to start eating again. Then as he went to put the knife and fork into his steak or whatever, Frank would pump the pumper and the damn plate would move all over the table.

We used to kill ourselves laughing. When you're 22 years of age and 24, and on your first tour of England you do see a funny side to things that you mightn't think so funny 30 years later.

But on a long tour like 1961 it was vitally important that you retained your sense of humour. There were 17 of us, so six were always going to be disappointed at missing Test selection and it was vital that they stayed a happy bunch.

Certainly the fun and games helped to make the trip more

> **Bill Lawry had his head sliced open by a bumper from South African fast bowler Peter Pollock at Durban in 1966–67. He retired hurt to receive 10 stitches but returned to top score with 44 in Australia's total of 147.**

enjoyable for Lindsay Kline, Barry Jarman and Ian Quick, who all missed out on playing in a Test match.

Because Syd was a QC he was also strict about the team getting down on time for travel to the grounds, and he was also a great one for protocol, so a tour of England was really the perfect one for Syd to indulge himself.

He liked to tell us if he had an important engagement any day. He would come bustling into the group and say, "Good morning Richie, good morning boys." Then he would go into detail.

"Big day for us today boys. At lunchtime I'm required to go over to the club dining rooms. Lord De L'Isle is coming as a guest of the club and I'm going to be the guest of honour."

"I've got my speech prepared. It's all written down in here," and he would tap the little attaché case he used to carry with him everywhere.

It had two handles and a top that folded out, more box-like than peak-shaped like a briefcase.

Syd would continue, "I'm very confident you know. I'll do a good job for you boys." And we'd say, "Very good Syd. That's great and you can be sure we'll be doing our best for you out on the field." It was something of a ritual.

On one particular occasion we arrived at a ground and Syd, after placing his case on a bench in the dressingroom, went about his usual procedure, which was to walk out into the middle of the ground and inspect the pitch.

Then he and the team treasurer, Ray Steele, would go to the turnstiles to see they were clicking over satisfactorily, then return to the rooms, where Syd would announce, "Well, we've done all that, Ray and I are now going over to the Members'."

When Syd had put his case down on the bench I saw Frank Misson's eyes fairly light up and while Syd went on his walkabout Frank climbed up on the table, stepped across to the window sill, which was higher, and tossed a rope across the rafters of the dressingroom. It was a very high roof, believe me.

Frank attached one end of the rope to the case, then pulled on the rope until the case was just brushing against a rafter. He was a good six-footer Frank, and he fixed the other end of the rope just out of the reach of any person of average height.

Syd, back from his rounds, headed for where he'd left his case. "Where's my bag? Where's my bag," he demanded. No one was game to say a thing, and we all just stood there with smirks on our faces and giving the odd shrug of our shoulders.

Finally Syd's eyes went to the heavens and he saw his case and shouted "I'll kill you Misson, I'll kill you!"

As long as I live I will never forget the sight of Syd trying to get his case down.

His pants always seemed too short anyway, because he was fat around the girth, but now he was up on the trestle table, which was swaying slightly, broom in an upstretched arm trying to knock his case over the rafter. It must have taken him an hour to get it down and by that time we had been laughing so much we had tears in our eyes.

I've got no idea what happened in the cricket that day, but I do know that as far as team spirit was concerned the 1961 tour of England was one of the most successful ever.

My friend Frank Misson, and Syd Webb, however reluctantly, were certainly the leaders in that department.

Chapter Five

Greg Chappell

Born 1948, Gregory Stephen Chappell, the middle of three brothers, Ian and Trevor being the others, a hat trick that inevitably drew comparisons with England's famous Grace family.

He left just as indelible a mark on world cricket as did his elder brother Ian, and had it not been for the notorious 'Underarm incident' off the last ball of a World Series Cup match in 1981, Greg's legacy would have been less controversial.

There was a majesty about Greg Chappell's strokeplay; tall, cool and composed under pressure from the great fast bowlers of his era, he favoured the drive as his main scoring shot.

He began his Test career against England at the WACA ground in Perth—which coincidentally was also making its Test 'debut'—and immediately went into the record books by scoring a century. There were 23 more to come.

He also scored a century in his last Test, against Pakistan, an innings of 182 that not only took him past 7000 runs in Test cricket, but took him past Sir Donald Bradman's run record.

And, just for good measure, in his first Test after taking on the captaincy handed over by his brother Ian in 1975–76 he hit a century in each innings against the West Indies—and hit the runs that won the Test!

Six of his centuries were against Pakistan, a record against that country he shares with Allan Border, who has since passed Chappell's Test run-scoring aggregate.

But the century he holds highest in his personal record was his 131 at Lord's in 1972, which he recalls as his best technically. "I only made one mistake—when I played on to D'Oliveira," he says.

By now you may be thinking there is an ice-cool ruthlessness to Greg Chappell's cricket, and that may not be far from the truth. Ian likens him to Bjorn Borg, the 'Iceman' of tennis.

Greg was the 35th Australian captain, and admits that sometimes the pressures of the job became too demanding, particularly about the time of the split between 'official' cricket and the cricket promoted by Kerry Packer.

Although Greg Chappell began his first-class career with South Australia, he finished it with Queensland where he was able to establish himself in business, thus ensuring a life after cricket.

However, he did retain a close involvement in the game; he became a highly-placed administrator with Queensland and was elected to the national selection panel, a role he filled at one of the most difficult times in Australian cricket history.

When Greg Chappell scored 247 not out and 133 in a Test against New Zealand at Wellington in 1973–74 his aggregate of 380 runs was the most in a single Test—England's Andy Sandham scored 375 against the West Indies in 1930.

TEST RECORD

Batting

Opponents	Debut	M	Inn	N.O	Runs	H.S	50	100	Avrge
England	1970/71	36	65	8	2619	144	12	9	45.95
India	1980/81	3	5	–	368	204	2	1	73.60
New Zealand	1973/74	14	22	3	1076	*247	3	3	56.63
Pakistan	1972/73	17	27	2	1581	235	6	6	63.24
Sri Lanka	1982/83	1	1	–	66	66	1	–	66.00
West Indies	1972/73	17	31	5	1400	*182	7	5	53.85
Total		88	151	18	7110	*247	31	24	53.46

Bowling

Opponents	Debut	M	Ball	Mdns	Runs	Wkts	Avrge	5	Best	Stk/Rt	RPO	Eco/Rt
England	1970/71	36	1867	70	679	13	52.23	–	2/36	143.62	2.18	36.37
India	1980/81	3	120	10	27	1	27.00	–	1/4	120.00	1.35	22.50
New Zealand	1973/74	14	1314	43	462	13	35.54	_	3/54	101.08	2.11	35.16
Pakistan	1972/73	17	1082	37	418	12	34.83	1	5/61	90.17	2.32	38.63
Sri Lanka	1982/83	1	6	–	2	–	–	–	–	–	2.00	33.33
West Indies	1972/73	17	938	48	325	8	40.63	–	2/10	117.25	2.08	34.65
Total		88	5327	208	1913	47	40.70	1	5/61	113.34	2.15	35.91

AT THE SELECTION TABLE

by Greg Chappell

One of the decisions you must make when you retire after spending a long time in first-class cricket is whether or not you are prepared to put something back into the game.

To me, taking on the role of a national selector was a constructive way to stay involved in the game, and it was also a challenge. And I felt that if I was going to do it then

> *Greg Chappell passed the half-century 55 times in Tests. In his 151 Test innings he was never out in the 90s, once being 98 not out. He made 13 ducks in his 88 Tests. His four first-class double-centuries were all made in Tests. He hit 24 centuries.*

I would have the most to offer immediately upon my retirement from the game, simply because I would still be in touch, so to say.

I wasn't worried that I mightn't be able to handle it. Playing and captaincy had given me the necessary experience for the job, and there was a period during my captaincy when I was a selector too.

That can be a tough situation. While I personally felt I had something to offer wearing the two hats I also felt it could lead to conflict.

If a captain is going to be a selector he needs the whole-hearted support of not just his fellow selectors, but most importantly his team. It was particularly so in a case where a player was dropped.

He and his mates could be forgiven for thinking the captain was directly responsible, or didn't offer enough support in the selection room, thus causing problems with team morale. If the individual was chosen again later in the season it was distinctly possible his confidence in the captain could be affected.

Some may see a similar predicament facing the current coach Bob Simpson in his dual role as a coach and selector.

My time as a selector, from 1984 to 1988, coincided with a transition period in Australian cricket, and it was therefore not a particularly easy time, but a most important time.

A handful of experienced players had retired in the early eighties and the South African rebel tours had drained a large number of the experienced first season Sheffield Shield players who may have bridged the gap. This created problems for the selectors because it effectively widened the gap between the standard of Sheffield Shield cricket and Test cricket.

It has long been my belief that a player needs at least two, maybe three or four seasons in Shield cricket before he is ready for Test cricket—an apprenticeship if you like. However it is becoming more difficult for selectors to adhere to that policy in these fast-track recent times.

Media pressure, even administrative pressure in the form of coaches or prominent officials, has a tendency to push the new, young players very hard. Selectors, who usually prefer to take longer to digest talent, can come in for some heavy criticism if they don't bow to the push.

My point about the apprenticeship is that hopefully the player will have experienced a few low points in that period and learnt not just how to deal with them, but to fight back. Test cricket is not the place to suffer your first disappointments.

Unfortunately, with the loss of so many to South Africa we were forced to blood some players before they had had the benefit of this learning period. Two examples of players who suffered this fate were Steve Waugh and Craig McDermott.

In the circumstances their outstanding talent demanded they be chosen, but both suffered their first real setbacks at the Test level and they struggled to survive. It is a credit to both of them that they were able to overcome these early setbacks and go on to establish themselves in the Test and limited-overs arenas.

Under Laurie Sawle's chairmanship a selection philosophy of giving players time to learn how to play Test cricket was reinforced. At any given time in Australian cricket I believe there are only 15 or so players with the ability, temperament and commitment to be successful at the highest level of the game.

These players must be given every opportunity to learn what international cricket is all about. This can take two to three seasons depending on the player. The more talent he has the more opportunities he is likely to be given.

To achieve this the selectors are often required to come up with a neat balancing act, and that is not always appreciated by the followers of the game, even by some of the players.

This was especially the case in the mid-eighties for the reasons already mentioned. Consequently quite a few players were chosen, but some were discarded quickly when it was found they weren't up to it, or not quite ready.

But once the nucleus of the side was identified those players were given every opportunity to establish themselves. A few, like Waugh, McDermott and even David Boon were omitted from time to time to allow them to rehabilitate back in Shield cricket. This was so if we felt they had suffered a loss of form or a lapse in confidence.

The Test and limited-overs programme these days makes it doubly difficult for a player down on form.

Another problem during the transition period was the loss of Kim Hughes as captain. Kim had been elevated to the position before he was ready and had struggled with the job, and that had probably caused his own play to suffer.

The biggest problem, again for reasons touched on, was that Kim's most obvious replacement was Allan Border, who was reluctant to take it on because of his lack of preparation and experience for what had become a much more involved role than it once was.

I had been calling for some time for more support for the captain as the game was changing and the captaincy role becoming more demanding. Fortunately for Border the Cricket Board, after ignoring my pleas for a long time, moved to appoint a media manager and a cricket manager, now coach, to act as a buffer for the captain.

It all came too late for Kim Hughes, who was so shattered he slipped out of the side. There is no doubt Allan wouldn't have survived as long as he has without that support system in place.

That is a good thing for Australian cricket, for as scarce as Test cricketers are, captaincy material is even thinner on the ground.

The Kim Hughes saga didn't end there—at the end of that season he was left out of the touring party for England. Kim's form and confidence was at rock bottom and the belief at the time was that he needed a complete rest and time to rehabilitate with the view to having him available for the following season.

There was no doubt he would bounce back and be a valuable member of the Australian team. If he had been informed of this thinking he may not have accepted the offer to captain the rebel tour of South Africa.

Even he may agree now, with the benefit of hindsight, that he needed a break from the game.

Test cricket requires more than pure talent. Temperament and commitment to success as an individual and as a team are almost more important prerequisites. It is up to the selectors to identify these players and give them the opportunities to succeed.

Chapter Six

Tony Greig

Born 1946, Anthony William Greig. The son of a Scottish father and a South African mother, he lived in South Africa until 1966 when he moved to Sussex, England where he was to play County cricket.

He was a dominating figure on a cricket field, not just because he was fair and handsome and six feet eight inches (186 centimetres) tall; he oozed aggression, and the tougher the state of the game, the more it seemed he flourished. Evidence of that is probably most simply stated by the fact that his Test match performances outweigh his career performances.

A challenge inevitably brought out his best; on debut for Sussex he scored a century, saving his side from annihilation by Lancashire. When Lillee and Thomson were running amok on a pacy Gabba pitch in 1974–75 it was Greig who strode to the middle, swinging his bat in circles like a windmill, and for five hours defied the deadly duo in scoring 110 and saving England, if not from defeat, certainly from acute embarrassment.

He was one of the first batsmen to choose to raise his bat from the ground in readiness before the bowler had released the ball, believing it to be an aid as he went about the business of crashing the ball high and straight, or over cover.

He was also a fiercely competitive bowler and, for his height, an outstanding slips fieldsman. Normally he bowled at a brisk medium pace, but at Port-of-Spain in Trinidad in 1973–74 he reacted to the slow, crumbling pitch by reverting to slower off-spin and returned match figures of 13/156, the best ever by an England bowler in the West Indies.

It was in the first Test of that series that Greig's intensely competitive nature got him into a spot of bother.

West Indian batsman Bernard Julien played the last ball of the second day back down the pitch, Greig picked it up and, seeing the non-striker Alvin Kallicharran (not out 142) out of his ground, threw down the stumps and appealed.

Kallicharran was given out and something close to all hell broke loose, with the claim being made that Kallicharran was merely walking off at the end of the day. Peace—and Kallicharran's not-out status—was restored after a lengthy after-stumps discussion, at which the appeal was withdrawn.

His tough, inspirational attitude to the game so impressed the England selectors they made him captain, but as with so many other of the world's cricket captains about the time of the mid-seventies, he ran into the rampaging West Indian fast-bowling machine and that took some of the gloss off his record.

After World Series Cricket, where he played for The Rest Of The World team, he settled in Australia, where he had a stint in the insurance business—"Get the Lion on the Line" was his successful slogan. He is now the executive vice-president of PBL Sports Marketing, a subsidiary of Kerry Packer's Nine Network.

TEST RECORD

Batting

Opponents	Debut	M	Inn	N.O	Runs	H.S	50	100	Avrge
Australia	1972	21	37	1	1303	110	10	1	36.19
India	1972/73	13	18	2	883	148	5	3	55.19
New Zealand	1973	5	6	–	267	139	2	1	44.50
Pakistan	1972/73	6	9	–	351	72	2	–	39.00
West Indies	1973	13	23	1	795	148	1	3	36.14
Total		58	93	4	3599	148	20	8	40.44

Bowling

Opponents	Debut	M	Ball	Mdns	Runs	Wkts	Avrge	5	Best	Stk/Rt	RPO	Eco/Rt
Australia	1972	21	3472	114	1663	44	37.80	–	4/53	78.91	2.87	47.90
India	1972/73	13	2070	96	759	27	28.11	1	5/24	76.67	2.20	36.67
New Zealand	1973	5	849	23	361	20	18.05	2	5/51	42.45	2.55	42.52
Pakistan	1972/73	6	949	33	477	14	34.07	–	4/86	67.79	3.02	50.26
West Indies	1973	13	2462	72	1281	36	35.58	3	8/86	68.39	3.12	52.03
Total		58	9802	338	4541	141	32.21	6	8/86	69.52	2.78	46.33

FIELDS OF DREAMS

by Tony Greig

I grew up in Queenstown in South Africa, not a big place with a population of somewhere between 5000 and 10,000, but perfect for me because I was able to satisfy my great love of the outdoor life.

Our house was a big, rangy, single-storey place with spacious rooms that let the breezes circulate, a huge lawn flanked by trees, and lovely gardens.

It was the base for the family, my father Sandy, mother

Joyce and four children; it was the centrepiece of my youth, days I'll never forget, no matter what.

Both my mother and father had good sporting instincts; Mum played hockey, tennis and squash and Dad used to coach rugby. The Christmas holiday break was spent at a seaside place called Kei Mouth where I enjoyed an unorthodox form of cricket.

One of the relatives who came to Kei Mouth was an uncle, 'Dummy' Taylor, whose nickname came about as a result of his talent at rugby. He was a great competitor, always wanting to be in one thing or another.

At Kei Mouth it was balcony cricket which we played, naturally enough, on the balcony of the cottage with a tennis ball and a stump for a bat. To score you had to hit the ball between a host of pillars. Games would go on for hours, and each morning at sun up I'd race down to Dummy's place and wait for the day's play to begin.

There is a nine-year age difference between my brother Ian and I. When I was 14 years old and he was a small five-year-old I introduced him to 'senior' cricket. It was perhaps a little early, perhaps a little unfair but entirely necessary.

I was bowling to a close friend, Paul Ensor. Ian was fielding. My friend kept complaining that I was bowling too fast, and after a while I got tired of it, so I informed him "my little brother could face me bowling at that speed".

Tony Greig's toughness shone through on two England tours to India. In 1972–73 at Bombay he scored 148 and with Keith Fletcher (113), current England cricket manager, he shared a stand of 254, England's highest for the fifth wicket in all Tests. In 1976 he batted 415 minutes for 103, then the fourth slowest-ever innings for England, now the eighth. It was his 49th Test, and when he had scored three runs he became the first England player to achieve the 3000 runs and 100 wickets Test double.

Paul disputed this. Ian, looking a little bewildered, was brought up from his fielding position and padded up. I took my long, long run, hurtled in and bowled flat out—a half volley which Ian played as calm as you like.

I don't know if that impromptu trial helped but it is a matter of record that Ian went on to play successfully with England's County teams Sussex and Surrey.

There was another chap who was a regular in our garden Test matches. His real name was Teki Manzi, but I just called him 'Tackies'.

He was a black African who came to the door one time looking for a job. All he was wearing was khaki shorts and an old pair of plimsolls, known in South Africa as tackies. Dad decided to make him the gardener. In fact he spent most of his time bowling to me in the garden!

Well, not so much bowling. In fact, Tackies was a chucker, and a very fast one at that. But he was an essential part of those make-believe Test matches of my boyhood.

In those matches my friends and I would choose to be five well-known cricketers; I always wanted as my five Ken Barrington, Colin Cowdrey, Peter May, Ted Dexter and Trevor Bailey, all Englishmen.

I would attempt to bat in a style like each of them, using whatever information I had gleaned by reading of their exploits. When I bowled I would 'take the new ball' as Brian Statham, then revert to the spin of Jim Laker. Some would find it significant that I ended up playing for England, and even bowling using those two methods, but I can assure you it was just a coincidence.

I scored my first 'real' century playing for Queen's College junior school against Cathcart, a smaller school from down the road. I remember the field was known as 'the bunny field', it was so tiny, and covered with rough grass.

My score was 130, and as a reward the owner of the local department store offered me a bat of my own choice. I chose not one of those autographed by a famous player, but one called 'The Barrier'.

It was a beauty because it lasted me for years, through every type of weather, against every type of cricket ball from the softest to the hardest.

Soon my weekends were wholly taken up with school sport. We'd get aboard the train at Queenstown on the Friday night and the adventure would begin. Nobody would sleep a wink and by midnight we would all be in one compartment of the train, having a feast and talking.

After the all-night trip we'd be met at our destination by the families of our opposition, who would take us home for breakfast, then get us to the game on time. After an all-day match they would treat us to supper before putting us back on the train for the all-night return trip.

I was already showing all-round talent, batting in the top order, bowling, seamers usually, and I would field anywhere, slips or outfield.

Yet it was on the strength of a rare turn at the crease bowling spin that won me a spot in the South African schoolboys squad for the first time. The pitch was wet and, thinking it would grip, I bowled some fast off-spin which got me seven or so wickets. That was a result I was to repeat later in my career, when I was playing for England.

I was also starting to make an impact as a captain, at various times being put in charge not just of the cricket team but also the tennis and rugby.

Big crowds, sometimes more than 2000 used to come to watch the rugby, and that lifted me. In my cricket career I

Tony Greig captained England in 14 Tests, won three, lost five, drew six; Mike Brearley took over from Greig in 1977. Greig made a 'duck' in his last Test innings for England, caught Bright bowled Malone, before joining Kerry Packer's World Series Cricket.

was often called "a big match player" and I won't argue with that. There does seem to be more point to a game when there's a big crowd present.

It was in rugby that I had my first significant success as a captain. I took over a losing team, but I believed the reason we had lost 15–0 to our arch rivals was not because we didn't have the ability but because we lacked the right spirit.

I worked on that for the return match. A big crowd was in and we turned on a great performance to win 11–3. Our coach summed it up when he said, "Our spirit was magnificent. It made all the difference."

A team can have all the ability in the world but if it doesn't have a happy spirit to make it a happy family then success will be hard to come by.

I was doing well enough at school for there to be discussions about me going on to university and eventually becoming a history teacher in my native Queenstown. History was my favourite subject.

A sudden illness, missed exams and a particularly successful time as a cricketer in my final years at school changed all that. I had done well enough to challenge hard for a spot in the South African Schools team which was to play a Provincial team, Griqualand West.

I was drafted into the team, but only in the place of Mike Procter, who had been punished by officials for some misdemeanour. But it was the beginning of my senior cricket career. The next season I again made the team, this time playing against Western Province, captained by the then captain of South Africa, Peter van der Merwe.

By the end of the season I was playing with Border Province in the B section of the Currie Cup, South Africa's equivalent of the Sheffield Shield. Then came another twist.

In my final year at school I achieved a pass mark good enough to get me into university, but delayed my entrance so I could do my year of compulsory National Service. I was

> *Tony Greig played 58 Tests consecutively, the most*
> *by an England player. He is one of only nine players*
> *in Test cricket to score 1000 runs, take 50 wickets*
> *and hold 50 catches, an honour he shares with*
> *Richie Benaud.*

rejected, probably on the grounds of my epilepsy, and so found myself with a spare year. What to do?

It just so happened the cricket coach at Queen's was Mike Buss, the allrounder from the England County team Sussex. I approached him with the proposition that Sussex might have a spot for me for the following English season.

Mike wrote to Sussex and after what seemed like an eternity the reply came. They made the point that I didn't have a sensational record at school, however if I was prepared to pay my fare over they would give me a year's trial at £15 a week.

I travelled by boat and on docking at Southampton was met by the Sussex secretary, Colonel P C Williams. On the long drive to Hove Colonel Williams told me he expected it to be a gloriously hot summer, and in reply to my query explained, with a wave of a hand at the leafless trees, that his prediction was based on the height of the crows' nests.

Once the season got started it was, but April, when I arrived, was an appalling month. So keen was I to get going I took a ball out to the nets and bowled—onto thick snow! It was an event that amused a couple of Sussex players observing me from behind fogged window panes.

As the summer lengthened so did the odds of my returning home for another three years to study history at university. My destiny was settled when Sussex offered me a three-year contract.

I worked during the English winter in the family department store complex, Greig's, in Scotland, mostly in the electrical area delivering, installing and collecting television sets which were rented out.

There was one part of the job that I hated: if a family failed to pay the rent over a period of time, I was sent out to retrieve the set. I witnessed some heart-breaking scenes, and I wasn't sorry when that role finished.

In the first match of my first season under contract I scored 156, after being perilously close to leg before first ball to Brian Statham, the bowler I had tried to copy all those years before in the garden Tests in Queenstown.

And later in the season I turned in the bowling figures that were to remain my career's best: 8 for 25 against Gloucester. But overall I'd describe my success as only moderate.

When I had discussed whether I should take the three-year contract with my father he had hesitated, in the end agreeing that if at the end of that time I hadn't made it then I would have to get out and find a job with more security.

In 1970 the scheduled tour to England by a team from South Africa was cancelled; in their place came a Rest Of The World team which won the First Test by an innings.

The England selectors made five changes for the Second Test, and among the newcomers—me!

There was much resentment the length and breadth of England that some brash young fellow with a South African accent was taking a spot in the national team.

But I was eligible through residence and through my father's birthplace, Scotland. I yearned to do well, to justify my selection, to silence the critics who I knew were hovering, hoping that I would muck it all up.

Chapter Seven

The Infamous Underarm

The 'Underarm incident' took place at the MCG in front of 52,990 fans on February 1, 1981. It happened because New Zealand were within cooee of pulling off a momentous tie with Australia.

With one ball to go in the match the scores were: Australia 4/235, New Zealand 8/229. A six would tie it—but Greg Chappell, Australia's captain, reasoned there wasn't a batsman in the world who'd manage that if he told the bowler, his brother Trevor, to send one down underarm.

It created an international incident. The New Zealand prime minister said yellow was the right colour for the Australians to be wearing. It stirred jokes about deodorants labelled "Chappell".

An administrator admonished Greg Chappell with the observation delivered near to tears: "You may have won the game son, but you've lost a lot of friends."

But Doug Walters, whose sense of humour rose to the surface no matter how deep any crisis, said, "Fifty thousand people left the MCG today feeling just like I did when I saw the movie The Sting. They were shaking their heads asking 'What the hell happened there!' "

GREG CHAPPELL

The Underarm incident was not as cold and calculating as most critics would have you believe. Instead it was the culmination of frustrations that had built up over a long time, anger from my dissatisfaction in general with things cricket, but in particular anger over conditions at the MCG.

It was 1981, and in my opinion the second innings of the Centenary Test against England, in 1977, was about the last good pitch I'd played on at the MCG.

Through the late seventies and early eighties there were many occasions when I had discussions with the Victorian Cricket Association and the Australian Cricket Board, with umpires and visiting captains, about the inadequate pitch conditions at the MCG.

But no one seemed to be listening. The usual answer was, "Well, it's the same for both teams." Unfortunately that over-simplified a situation which was just not satisfactory for the showplace of Australian cricket—the MCG is to Australian

WATCH OUT - THEY'RE BRINGING ON THEIR UNDERARM BOWLER..!

cricket what Lord's is to English cricket.

The MCG is our most visible, and most supported venue; but the poor conditions made it difficult for players to turn on the sort of excellent cricket we believed we could and the paying public were being short-changed. In my eyes it was a tragedy.

It was a struggle to make scores in the low 200s in limited-overs matches, yet I believed the teams had the players capable of making 300–plus totals. One-day cricket is about runs, and the public want to see runs flowing, not batsmen struggling to make them.

Also, it was the time just after World Series Cricket began, when the game was going through a transition period.

The media were a lot more interested in the fortunes of Australian cricketers than ever before. I can remember getting phone calls as early as 5.30 a.m. and as late as midnight, reporters wanting statements for their radio news bulletins. It wasn't so bad on tour when I could have the hotel receptionist block the calls, but at home not even a silent number stopped them.

Reporters became so hungry for angles to their stories some actually booked themselves into the team hotels so they could ring on the internal system, bypassing the receptionist. Some would even come and knock on my door at dawn.

And on an administrative level there were policy meetings that the Australian captain had to attend in that period. Sometimes they would be after a day's play, sometimes on rest days, subcommittee meetings that were time consuming and added to the pressures.

The Underarm incident was, I suppose you could say, a cry for help.

At that stage I believed I had made every reasonable effort to try to get the situation improved for the Australian captain. But the administrators didn't seem to be interested, probably because they didn't realise the enormity of the problem.

I'd have to say not even those teammates I was closest to in the Australian side were aware how tough the going had become. I can't blame them for that, because I don't think even I fully understood what I was going through.

On the day of the Underarm, the third match in the final series, there was some poor cricket by the Australian team. We had got ourselves into a position where we couldn't lose the game, but New Zealand could tie it.

If they did that, by hitting a six off the last ball of the match, that would have taken my team into an extra one-day match before the final Test—the sixth of the summer— against India at the MCG a week later.

I certainly didn't need an extra game and the senior players, who had played in all the games, certainly didn't need an extra game. We just needed a few days off.

I was sitting on the ground at deep mid-on when New Zealand's last man, Brian McKechnie, walked through the gate. I was trying to wind down, trying to relax, but I realised that if anyone was likely to hit the ball out of the MCG, a big ask but possible, then McKechnie could. He was a big strong fellow.

My brother Trevor was to bowl—if he bowled the ball in the wrong place, who knows?

I just snapped.

I was mentally unfit to be captain of the side at that stage and on that day it all came down on me.

The biggest frustration for me, I suppose, was that nobody seemed to understand what was going on. I still regret the incident, and always will. I would never try to excuse myself, or anyone else, for doing it or having done it.

I can only hope history will judge me more evenly than the commentators did at the time.

> *Ian and Greg Chappell figured in six century
> partnerships for Australia. Simpson and Lawry were
> together in nine, and Greg Chappell and Kim Hughes
> matched Woodfull and Bradman with seven.*

IAN CHAPPELL

I disagreed with the Underarm, because I don't believe in conceding to the opposition that one of their players might be better than one of yours.

I also thought it was most unfair on Trevor.

I expressed those sentiments in a column following the match. I next ran into Greg after I'd parked my car on the SCG number two ground before the last final against New Zealand. At the same time as I pulled up, a bus carrying band members for the pre-game entertainment parked near the practice nets.

As I walked past the Australian team on my way to the commentary box, I said hello to Greg.

"Thought you would've come on the bus," answered Greg.

"I have my own car Greg," I replied, "why would I want to come by bus?"

"Because you jumped on the bandwagon, just like the rest of them," he growled.

"If you don't like what I write, then don't read it," I answered.

There was a hint of a smile; "Anyway, it's probably just as well you did disagree," said Greg. "Trevor bowled it, I ordered it and if you'd agreed with it, they would have thought we were all mad."

That's the last conversation we've had on the subject.

BILL LAWRY

At the time of the Underarm Ian Chappell and I were on air for Channel Nine's *Wide World of Sports* and I was the ball-to-ball commentator. In those dying moments of what was an exciting game, when Greg Chappell called his brother Trevor up to bowl, it became apparent by the long, animated discussion between captain and bowler that something unusual was going to happen.

I actually predicted at the time that they were going to bowl an underarm. Of course, when it happened the match ended in tremendous drama and controversy.

For me, one of the saddest moments came afterwards when, walking down the back of the Members' Stand at the MCG I saw some of the old members actually had tears in their eyes. They felt that the game of cricket had been terribly tainted. And it certainly did nothing for relationships between New Zealand and Australia!

But the fact was that the underarm was a legal delivery at the time; it was allowed by the laws of cricket and Greg Chappell, or any other captain, had the right to bowl underarm at any time during any cricket match, provided he indicated to the umpire and the opposing batsmen that the bowl was to change from overarm to underarm.

On reflection I guess that Greg Chappell, if he had his time over, would possibly not have brought on Trevor Chappell to bowl an underarm, but you have to understand the enormous stress that the captain and players are put under in today's marketplace.

There's always going to be some type of controversy, whether it be underarm or bodyline or bouncers, whenever and wherever the game is played. And we all, in our moments of excitement and pressure and controversy, forget that at the end of the day cricket is only a game.

TONY GREIG

There can be absolutely no doubt that this unsavoury incident will be spoken of in conjunction with the name Greg Chappell for as long as cricket exists. It was an unsporting act perpetrated in trying circumstances by a strong character.

A chat with any Kiwi will unearth a blow by blow recital of the incident and a few reasons why every living Australian cricketer should be hung, drawn and quartered.

But to brand Greg with this isolated incident forever is very unfair when one considers the great joy he brought to so many cricket lovers. His majestic batting style was a pleasure to watch. His slip catching was as good as any I've ever seen and to add to all that he was a fine medium-pace bowler, albeit his temperament was not really suited to bowling.

On a positive note on the Underarm, it could be argued that any cricketer who was either good enough, or astute enough, to exploit the laws of one of the oldest games of all to the extent that the laws had to be changed to accommodate any repetition has made a positive contribution to the game of cricket.

Another example concerned Don Bradman who was so good that the English fast bowlers were persuaded to resort to 'bodyline' bowling tactics. In so doing they halved Bradman's batting average but forced a change to the laws

Tony Greig captained England in the Centenary Test at the MCG in March, 1977. Australia won by 45 runs, exactly the same margin as in the very first Test 100 years earlier. But the Test was also memorable for a brief passage of play when debutant batsman David Hookes, in one over, hit Greig's fastish off-spin for five consecutive boundaries.

about the number of fieldsmen allowed behind the square leg umpire—which was a compliment to Bradman's batting skill, Larwood's bowling and the tactical ability and resolve of England's captain, Douglas Jardine.

The incident most comparable to Greg's underarm ploy was when Mike Brearley, England's captain, played all his fieldsmen on the boundary in a limited-overs International in an effort to ensure that the Australians could not win. This move also resulted in a change of the laws—to incorporate the 'circles' in one-day cricket.

Thankfully, Brearley's tactic and the underarm are no longer an option. So rest in peace Greg Chappell!

Chapter Eight

On Top Down Under

There have been 38 Australian cricket captains, although five of them only got to toss the coin once—Hugh Hamon Massie, William Alfred Brown, Raymond Russell Lindwall, Neil Robert Harvey and Barrington Noel Jarman.

Ten of them never lost a Test, three of them never won a toss. Captains' roles off the field have been varied: accountant, stockbroker, solicitor, pharmacist, plumber, dentist, crime reporter, schoolmaster.

Batsmen have been most favoured for the job, particularly high-order batsmen. Allrounders and spin bowlers have been moderately popular, but fast bowlers and wicketkeepers have rarely got the nod.

Most Test captains have hailed from New South Wales and Victoria, then South Australia. Western Australia has had but one, Kim Hughes.

This chapter is about captains from Down Under. But for the record the reader might be interested in the captaincy records of our other two commentators who led from the front, but from beneath the England cap.

Tony Greig captained England 14 times, won three, lost five, drew six. David Gower captained England 32 times, won five, lost 18 and drew nine.

Australian Test Captaincy Records

Captain	Tests as captain	Eng	Ind	NZ	Pak	SAf	SL	WI	Won	Lost	Drwn	Tie	Won Toss
DW Gregory	3	3	—	—·	—	—	—	—	—	2	1	—	—	2
WL Murdoch	16	16	–	–	–	–	–	–	–	5	7	4	–	7
TP Horan	2	2	–	–	–	–	–	–	–	–	2	–	–	1
HH Massie	1	1	–	–	–	–	–	–	–	1	–	–	–	1
JM Blackham	8	8	–	–	–	–	–	–	–	3	3	2	–	4
HJH Scott	3	3	–	–	–	–	–	–	–	–	3	–	–	1
PS McDonnell	6	6	–	–	–	–	–	–	–	1	5	–	–	4
G Giffen	4	4	–	–	–	–	–	–	–	2	2	–	–	3
GHS Trott	8	8	–	–	–	–	–	–	–	5	3	–	–	5
J Darling	21	18	–	–	–	–	3	–	–	7	4	10	–	7
H Trumble	2	2	–	–	–	–	–	–	–	2	–	–	–	1
MA Noble	15	15	–	–	–	–	–	–	–	8	5	2	–	11
C Hill	10	5	–	–	–	–	5	–	–	5	5	–	–	5
SE Gregory	6	3	–	–	–	–	3	–	–	2	1	3	–	1
WW Armstrong	10	10	–	–	–	–	–	–	–	8	–	2	–	4
HL Collins	11	8	–	–	–	–	3	–	–	5	2	4	–	7
W Bardsley	2	2	–	·	–	–	–	–	–	–	–	2	–	1
J. Ryder	5	5	–	–	–	–	–	–	–	1	4	–	–	2
WM Woodfull	25	15	–	–	–	5	–	–	5	14	7	4	–	12
VY Richardson	5	–	–	–	–	–	5	–	–	4	–	1	–	1
DG Bradman	24	19	5	–	–	–	–	–	–	15	3	6	–	10
WA Brown	1	–	–	1	–	–	–	–	–	1	–	–	–	–
AL Hassett	24	10	–	–	–	–	10	–	4	14	4	6	–	18
AR Morris	2	1	–	–	–	–	–	–	1	–	2	–	–	2
IW Johnson	17	9	2	–	1	–	–	–	5	7	5	5	–	6
RR Lindwall	1	–	1	–	–	–	–	–	–	–	–	1	–	–
ID Craig	5	–	–	–	–	5	–	–	–	3	–	2	–	3
R Benaud	28	14	5	–	3	1	–	–	5	12	4	11	1	11
RN Harvey	1	1	–	–	–	–	–	–	–	1	–	–	–	–
RB Simpson	39	8	10	–	2	9	–	–	10	12	12	15	–	20
BC Booth	2	2	–	–	–	–	–	–	–	–	1	1	–	1
WM Lawry	26	10	7	–	–	4	–	–	5	9	8	9	–	7
BN Jarman	1	1	–	–	–	–	–	–	–	–	–	1	–	1
IM Chappell	30	16	–	6	3	–	–	–	5	15	5	10	–	17
GS Chappell	48	15	3	8	9	–	–	1	12	21	13	14	–	29
GN Yallop	7	6	–	–	1	–	–	–	–	1	6	–	–	6
KJ Hughes	28	6	6	–	9	–	–	–	7	4	13	11	–	13
AR Border	78	23	11	14	6	–	6	18	24	19	34	1	41
Total	525	275	51	29	34	53	7	77	214	149	160	2	260

IAN CHAPPELL

The captaincy of Australia is a great honour, but it can wear you out mentally. It's not an 11 to 6 job and my intense approach left me in no fit mental state to back up to the West Indies in 1975–76, following the World Cup and a four-Test series in England in 1975.

I felt it was going to be a tough series against Clive Lloyd's men, and the only way Australia was going to win was by attacking the Windies. I felt my staleness would hinder my thinking and hurt Australia, so I retired from the captaincy. I stayed on to play that series because I didn't want anybody accusing me of walking away from a confrontation with the West Indies pacemen.

The job of captaining Australia really hasn't changed much if you do it properly. The first priority is to your players and to ensure you get the best out of them, so that you perform well as a team.

I think the most important job for a modern captain is to plan his time and get his priorities right. There are greater commitments to media and sponsors now, but a captain must remember that he is no good without having 10 players who are behind him all the way. The players come first and the sponsors and the media tie for second.

I've heard suggestions about using one captain for the Tests and one for the limited-overs matches.

If the man you've chosen to lead the side can't fathom the difference in the two games, then you've got the wrong bloke. A good cricketer is a good cricketer whether he's playing for one day, or four or five days. The same applies to a captain. The reason they are good is because they are

Ian Chappell scored Test cricket's 1000th century, 165 against the West Indies at the MCG in 1978–79.

skilful and smart enough to adapt their skills to the requirements of the game.

The enjoyment in captaincy is derived from getting the best out of a team of different personalities. I didn't believe in curfews, because if you treat players as adults, they will get to know what works best for them and prepare for the important matches accordingly. If you have selectors why do you need a curfew?

I believe there's a tendency in a lot of sports to put too much emphasis on conforming and not enough on performing. It is nonsensical to expect all players to prepare for a game in the same manner. If you have Doug Walters imitating an owl and hootin' and hollerin' at night, Dennis Lillee impersonating 'Deek' and doing miles and miles in training and Rodney Marsh who is likely to be teetotal for five days, then a totally dedicated drinker for the next three, how can you ask them to all conform to the same set of rules?

My fondest memory as captain of Australia was winning the Ashes at the SCG in 1974–75. When Geoff Arnold was caught off the bowling of Ashley Mallett to give us a three–nil lead with two Tests remaining, Rod Marsh raced over to me and as we were shaking hands he said, "We've got the bastards back."

England had held the Ashes since 1970–71 when they won them under Ray Illingworth's captaincy. Many of the Australian players were involved in that series, and after coming close to regaining the Ashes in England in 1972 it felt good to know that what we'd been responsible for losing, we'd now regained.

As much as anything I remember the celebration after we'd won at the SCG. It started in the dressingroom and it was pleasing to see the selectors, Neil Harvey, Phil Ridings and Sam Loxton, enjoy the victory as much as the players. I also remember Ian Redpath having his traditional glass of champagne with Rodney and cigarette with Doug Walters after an Australian victory. It was a very happy room and the party carried on at the 'Different Drummer' restaurant.

My final memory of the evening was Dennis Lillee walking around the 'Drummer' with a measuring bowl on his head singing the team song 'Under the Southern Cross'.

RICHIE BENAUD

There's so much cricket played now that the old style Commonwealth teams are no more; superseded, one might say. Ron Roberts, a highly respected English journalist, took several Commonwealth teams to Asia and Africa around the late 1950s and early 1960s, to spread the cricket message— a case of good fun as well as good will, if you like.

I was captain of two of them and there was a wide variety of players included, from many countries.

The late Ken Barrington, an outstanding England batsman in the fifties and sixties, was on one of the tours, and he pleaded with me to teach him to bowl the flipper so he could add it to his leg-spinning repertoire.

It is a very difficult ball to bowl as it is spun clockwise from underneath the wrist and it puts quite a strain on the tendons of the bowling hand. At any rate, after several sessions in the nets in Africa, Kenny went back to Surrey for their early-season practice, showed the flipper to his teammates and, by the time the third match came along, he was ready to bowl it for the first time in a match.

He told the wicketkeeper it would be the last ball of the over, ran up and bowled it; but unfortunately, a combination of nerves and cold fingers had it finish up a head-high full toss outside leg stump. The batsman smashed it past the helmetless Tony Lock's nose at short leg and it bounced

> *Richie Benaud was the bowler in one of cricket's most controversial dismissals. West Indian Joe Solomon was out "hit wicket" when his cap dislodged during a stroke and fell onto his stumps.*

twice and rocketed into the fence. 'Lockie' didn't blink and, as he and Kenny passed one another, Ken said, "Sorry mate, she slipped."

Lockie stood there, hands on hips, and announced loudly to the other players and spectators, "Bloody marvellous, i'n'it ... It took Benaud three years to perfect the flipper and Barrington's mastered it in three weeks!"

When Ron Roberts organised his tour of Africa, Asia, New Zealand and Hong Kong in the early 1960s, Doug Ford, the NSW 'keeper, was needed in New Zealand because the main 'keeper was injured. Doug was so popular the team decided to try to find some way to have him complete the tour. Cricketers are nothing if not inventive, and the players had a whiparound to the tune of £200, as the currency was then, and we placed it on a trotter at Addington on the Friday evening.

The price was 8/1, the information was 'hot' and, had it won, the winnings would just have covered the cost for Doug to travel with us to Hong Kong. It would be nice to say it won, but it didn't. It ran second and tried its heart out, but to no avail.

If you have occasionally wondered about the derivation of "diamond's are a skip's best friend" in cricket jargon, it came from the Hong Kong section of that tour. At the old Hong Kong cricket ground we made 240 in our innings and, with a judicious blend of skill and razzamatazz, I managed to get the local side past 200 against quite a formidable bowling attack. I then became over-confident and bowled Roy McLean and Everton Weekes for one over too many. The local batsmen, to the delight of the big crowd, smashed them all over the park and needed only two to win with three wickets in hand from the final over for a famous victory.

I said to Neil Adcock, the great South African fast bowler, as I handed him the ball, "We need a hat trick." He took the next three wickets in three balls.

We were walking off the field when I caught sight of Harold 'Dusty' Rhodes, the England fast bowler who was one of our team. He was puce in the face. He shook his head at me and said, "Benordy, if you put your head into a bucket of slops you'd come up with a mouthful of diamonds ...!" Diamonds are not only a girl's best friend ...!

GREG CHAPPELL

Captaincy was something I never really had a burning ambition to do. I'd been captain of teams as a kid, but never harboured any ambition to be captain of my country.

But having got to play Test cricket, and having a brother, Ian, who was Australian captain, I did start to think about it, and once I realised I was a chance for the job it was one of my motives for moving to Queensland.

My reasoning was that if the chance to captain Australia came my way I'd be prepared for it via my experience as Queensland captain. Even so, I'd have to say my relative indifference towards the job in my youth meant I was perhaps not as deeply committed to captaincy as I could have been.

In fact, when Kerry Packer started up World Series Cricket, at which time I'd been captain of Australia for a couple of years, I was quite happy to hand the reins back to Ian. Captaincy hadn't grabbed me so hard that I wanted to fight someone for the job, especially someone I thought better qualified anyway.

Ian and I did our captaincy stints in differing periods of the game. Ian was captain when the 'old ways' still existed— no limited-overs games to speak of, just Test matches and the Sheffied Shield, and certainly no media hype.

I did most of my captaincy after World Series Cricket and the Australian Cricket Board had mended the fences, the beginning of what might be termed the 'Super-heroes of Cricket' era. Television and the mass media had made the players much more recognisable, and as a result there were more demands on the players' rest time, especially after a day's play, for interviews and so on.

I never had a problem with being a captain on the field, but there were times off the field when I felt I had lost control; I felt the Cricket Board allowed the media to have me on the end of a string.

At the end of a day's play, instead of being able to go and have a few beers with my teammates or the opposition players, I was in a media conference for anything up to an hour, and by the time I got back to the rooms most of the players had drifted off, or moved off to do interviews in their own right.

All this meant a loss of contact between captain and players. One of the most common criticisms of my captaincy style was that I wasn't as good a communicator, or man manager, as Ian was. I accept that. We are two very different individuals, he being more outgoing and I more introverted, on the surface anyway.

Ian did a fair bit of communicating over a few beers after

Ian and Greg Chappell have been the only brothers to both captain Australia; their grandfather, Victor Richardson, also captained Australia. Ian Chappell sent England in in his first Test as captain, but lost. Greg sent his opponents in 14 times in 48 Tests, winning eight and losing three.

play; I've never asked him, but in thinking about that I believe he would have found captaincy more difficult in the period after World Series.

Post World Series the Australian captain was also on a lot of Board subcommittees: there was the Players' Committee, the Captains' Committee and the captain was heavily involved in discussions about itineraries and season formats, playing conditions, tour conditions and so on.

The amount of cricket to be played seemed to treble with the advent of a double Test series and the World Series Cup limited-overs schedule, in which Australia copped most of the 'double-headers'—a hell of a weekend for the players and the captain.

The pressures on the captain increased dramatically; it's not wrong to say I was perhaps something of a guinea pig—and in the end it got me, just as it got Kim Hughes.

I agitated hard with the Cricket Board to get the message across that if they didn't do something to ease these pressures on the captain they were going to go through captains faster than they could be produced.

Allan Border, with due respect to him, could not have survived without the changes I agitated for—more infrastructure in place, including the media manager, to ease the pressures on a captain.

Another criticism levelled at me as a captain was that I had a problem tolerating players of lesser ability. I disagree strongly with that.

Not only would I say I was never intolerant of a player of 'lesser ability', I'd say I don't think there were too many players of that so-called lesser ability.

I didn't see myself as a particularly gifted player, but the talents I did have I certainly made the most of. If I was intolerant at any time it was with players who were talented, or more talented than myself, who didn't realise that talent either through lack of belief in themselves, or lack of effort, and so didn't make the most of their opportunities.

My Test captaincy high points came in the 1982–83 season, winning back the Ashes in Australia, and then in New Zealand, where I consider I had my best game when we won the Christchurch Test by an innings.

Even Rod Marsh was moved to say it was some of the best captaincy of a side he had seen; coming from 'Bacchus' that was high praise indeed.

The low point? The 1977 tour to England when the World Series Cricket negotiations were going on in the background, making it impossible for me as the captain, and the players, to be fully focused.

BILL LAWRY

Australia was set to tour India and Pakistan as well in 1969–70, but the Pakistan leg was cancelled, resulting in the nomination of South Africa as an alternative.

South Africa had lost a tour by England the previous year when South African authorities adhered strictly to the laws of apartheid and refused to allow England allrounder, Basil D'Oliveira, a 'Cape coloured', into the country.

Australia agreed to tour, despite a demand from trade union leaders in Australia that the tour also be cancelled as a protest against apartheid.

So began one of the most arduous, and controversial, tours ever made by an Australian team.

The team left on October 15, 1969 from Sydney airport and the next day arrived in Ceylon, now Sri Lanka, for a two-week tour.

The India leg of the tour began on October 28, 1969, and the team arrived in Johannesburg, South Africa on January 2, 1970. They returned home on March 23, 1970, a tour of duty of five and a half months spanning three countries.

As it was, a request from South Africa for a fifth Test to be played was denied when several of the Australian players refused to agree to the terms.

The Australian team was: Bill Lawry (c), Ian Chappell (v-c), Alan Connolly, Eric Freeman, John Gleeson, Jock Irvine, Ray Jordan, Graham McKenzie, Ashley Mallett, Laurie Mayne, Ian Redpath, Paul Sheahan, Keith Stackpole, Brian Taber, Doug Walters.

The Fourth Test between Australia and South Africa at St George's Park, Port Elizabeth, from March 5 to 10, 1970, was South Africa's last before excommunication. They won by 323 runs, a record margin between those two countries, and wrapped up the series four–nil.

This was the scoreboard:

South Africa

B. A. Richards	c Taber b Connolly	81	c Chappell b Mayne	126
E. J. Barlow	c McKenzie b Connolly	73	c Stackpole b Walters	27
A. Bacher*	run out	17	hit wkt b McKenzie	73
R. G. Pollock	c Taber b Gleeson	1	b Mayne	4
B. L. Irvine	c Redpath b Gleeson	25	c Gleeson b Mayne	102
D. T. Lindsay #	c Taber b Connolly	43	b Connolly	60
H. R. Lance	b Mayne	21	run out	19
M. J. Procter	c Taber b Connolly	26	c Mayne b Gleeson	23
P. M. Pollock	not out	4	not out	7
P. H. J. Trimborn	b Connolly	0		
A. J. Traicos	c Taber b Connolly	2		
Extras	(B 4, LB 3, NB 11)	18	(LB 9, NB 20)	29
Total		311	(8 wickets declared)	470

Australia

K. R. Stackpole	c Barlow b Procter	15	b Procter	20
W. M. Lawry*	c Lindsay b Lance	18	c Lindsay b Barlow	43
I. R. Redpath	c Trimborn b Procter	55	c Balow b Procter	37
I. M. Chappell	c Procter b Trimborn	17	c Trimborn b Barlow	14
K. D. Walters	c Lindsay b Trimborn	1	b Procter	23
A. P. Sheahan	c Procter b P.M.Pollock	67	c Lindsay b Trimborn	46

Australia *(cont.)*

H. B. Taber #	lbw b Barlow	3	not out		30
L. C. Mayne	b Procter	13	c Lindsay b Procter		12
G. E. McKenzie	c Barlow b P.M.Pollock	0	c Lindsay b Procter		2
J. W. Gleeson	c Lindsay b P.M.Pollock	8	b Procter		0
A. N. Connolly	not out	2	c Bacher b Trimborn		3
Extras	(LB 3, W 1, NB 9)	13	(LB 2, NB 14)		16
Total		212			246

Australia

	O	M	R	W	O	M	R	W
McKenzie	27	7	66	0	20	3	72	1
Mayne	27	4	71	1	29	6	83	3
Connolly	28.2	9	47	6	36	3	130	1
Walters	9	1	19	0	5	2	14	1
Gleeson	32	9	90	2	30.2	5	142	1
Redpath					1	1	0	0

South Africa

	O	M	R	W	O	M	R	W
P. M. Pollock	14	12	46	3	1.1	0	2	0
Procter	25.1	11	30	3	24	11	73	6
Barlow	9	1	27	1	18	3	66	2
Lance	8	1	32	1	10	4	18	0
Trimborn	17	1	47	2	20.2	4	44	2
Traicos	3	1	17	0	14	5	21	0
Richards					3	1	6	0

Falls of Wickets

Wkt	SA 1st	A 1st	SA 2nd	A 2nd
1st	157	27	73	22
2nd	158	46	199	98
3rd	159	80	213	116
4th	183	82	279	130
5th	208	152	367	189
6th	259	177	440	207
7th	294	191	440	234
8th	305	195	470	243
9th	305	208	–	243
10th	311	212	–	246

South Africa won by 323 runs.

Tony Greig always likes to remind me of the four–nil thrashing South Africa gave my Australian team back in 1970. And sure, it was a great moment for Tony and all South Africans, but the result needs to be put into some sort of perspective, because the Cricket Board had made a very big ask of my team.

When we arrived in South Africa for the four-Test series over six weeks we were coming straight from a tour to India, where we had played five Tests in eight weeks.

Since 1970, I think it's been proven over and over again that if any side from any country can go to the subcontinent, particularly India, and win a Test series three–one, then that team has played very well. We did that.

We survived what is considered by many to be the toughest of all tours, physically and mentally. You're under pressure all the time, not just in the very hot, dry conditions, and on pitches that turn square, but from the masses of people who just love their cricket and continually put the cricketers under the microscope.

A tour to South Africa would be difficult in any era, but it was particularly difficult in 1970, not just because we'd had the hard slog of India beforehand, but because at that time South Africa were a very, very good team.

Everyone says now, "Well, you shouldn't have gone,"—but there was a bit more to the tour than just trying to win a Test series. About this time the anti-apartheid movement was getting up speed and South Africa were being more or less starved of cricket.

In fact, their previous Test series had been against Australia too, in 1967. So by going we were, I think, doing the right thing in trying to promote world cricket at what was a very difficult time.

And I count myself as very fortunate to have gone there to play a Test series against the great opening batsman Barry Richards—it was to be his only Test series—and the mighty

Pollock brothers, Peter the fast bowler who had given me a 10-stitch reminder of his pace in the Third Test on the 1967 tour, and his brother Graeme, the great left-hand batsman who was certainly at his peak in 1970 and scored 274 against us at Durban, the highest score by a South African in Tests.

The captain was Ali Bacher, who in recent times has done such a great job in getting South Africa back into world cricket. Not a super cricketer Ali, but he was certainly a very shrewd captain.

From a personal viewpoint it was very disappointing that we weren't capable of beating them; from a team viewpoint, despite suggestions that we shouldn't have gone, I don't think any of the players would say today they'd rather not have gone.

Keith Stackpole still talks about that day at Durban, the first day of the Second Test, when Barry Richards was 90 at lunch, then went on to make his century—his first in Tests— off just 116 balls.

Then Graeme Pollock came out and played like the great player he was and proved to be right through his career, up until he was 40 years of age when he was still playing successfully against the touring rebel sides of the eighties.

I certainly wouldn't say the 1970 tour of South Africa wasn't of great benefit to me as a person, because I think it enabled me to cope better with the frustrations of life in general.

Australian cricketers are superstitious about the score '87', supposedly because it is 'unlucky-13' from a hundred. There have been dismissals, or dropped catches, when 87 is on the scoreboard. Bill Lawry is one of 11 Australian batsmen to score 87 in a Test. Worse than that, he was not out 87 when Richie Benaud declared the innings closed! If not destining Lawry to a cricketing life of misfortune, Benaud may have at least caused him some worrying moments.

Chapter Nine

Birds of a Feather

Towards the end of March, 1973, on an outside court at Trinidad's Port-of-Spain sports club, Ian Chappell, captain of Australia's cricket team, was playing doubles tennis. Naturally he was playing aggressively.

A commentator might have called it this way: "... Chappell's backhand, under sliced, to Edwards' forehand, down the line wrong foots Chappell ..."

Indeed, it wrong-footed Chappell so badly he fell over trying to change direction. The result was a badly sprained ankle, and with the vital Third Test of the then all-square series against the West Indies due to start the next day that was bad news for Australia.

Chappell got back up and immediately began to hobble around the court, his face more wrinkled than usual as he fought the pain. He ordered one of the others in the group to "Get a bucket of ice!" from the club bar.

When it came back he stuck his foot in it. On the morning of the Test he couldn't walk without a bad limp, and in a few hours the Test was to begin on a pitch that was grey and already crumbly, ideal for the four spinners in the West Indies line-up, led as it was at that time by the great off-spinner Lance Gibbs.

How would the injured Chappell cope? He had a local physio tape his ankle—there was none travelling with the team—and batted down at No. 6, instead of his normal No. 3..

Anchored to the crease in the first innings he made only eight runs before lobbing a catch back to the bowler; in the second innings, ankle freer, he returned to No. 3 and made a cool 97, which in the end gave Australia enough breathing space to snatch one of Test cricket's greatest victories.

Those of his fellow cricketers who witnessed his bumbling doubles play against Ross Edwards and partner that morning in Trinidad 20 years ago will be happy to know Ian is now learning to appreciate the intricacies of the game, because these days tennis is his relaxation.

The pastime of Nine's cricket commentators are fascinating. Bill Lawry races pigeons, Richie Benaud cooks and David Gower enjoys the African continent for a good reason.

Greg Chappell has an interest in golf that gives a new and much more businesslike meaning to the '19th hole'.

BILL LAWRY

Yes, pigeons are my hobby. In fact they've been a lifelong hobby of all the Lawry males. I've been very fortunate that my pigeons have enabled me to make friends all around the world in South Africa, England, the West Indies and other countries where pigeon fanciers, who are not even cricket fanciers, have written to me or rung me up at my hotel and said, "Would you like to come out for dinner or come to a barbecue?"

Whereas Richie Benaud and Ian Chappell played golf in their moments away from cricket, pigeons were my relaxation, and now that I've stopped playing I suppose you could say they are my fulltime hobby.

To the uninitiated, pigeons are bred to a pedigree that goes back 50 or 60 years. In the case of the Lawry family our pigeons were handed down to my brother and me by my father.

Racing pigeons are far different from the pigeons you might see in city parks or flying around city buildings.

Our pigeons can live up to 15 years of age, even 20, and they normally breed up to 10 or 12 years of age. How long they are raced is up to the individual owners, but basically in Australia we don't race them much past three or four years of age.

The distance of racing can vary from 80 kilometres up to 950 kilometres. One of the fascinations of the hobby is the fact that you breed the racing pigeons from your own stock, rear them, home them, train them and finally race them.

People always ask, "Do you lose many?" Well, race losses depend greatly on the elements, such as changes in the weather (storms, fog), the human element (the odd bird is shot), and of course nature (hawks take a percentage of birds).

But year in year out most of the losses are because of inclement weather, although one of the factors in those losses can be the fitness, or type, of bird that is sent out by the fancier.

Pigeon racing is very competitive. There are some people who are ultra-keen and who strive every week to try to win the race, and there are those who just love the hobby and just love to see their birds get back home.

I guess I'm in the first category. I do put a lot of time into my birds, from breeding through to training to racing and I'm looking to try to win every race that my birds compete in. It doesn't happen, but that's my objective.

"How do they get home?" is the other question that's most often asked. Well, that's a bit of a mystery and even scientists have yet to convince anybody that they know how the birds get back home.

There's a home instinct for sure in the racing pigeon from a point from say 80 kilometres to 150 kilometres away from the loft, and the bird does do his level best to get home as quickly as possible by the quickest direct route.

People have different ideas about why a pigeon goes home—the sun, magnetic fields, good eyesight—but really we haven't got a clue.

I certainly haven't got a 100 percent clear idea how the pigeon gets his homing instinct so spot-on. When you consider that on some days there are seven or eight thousand birds coming into 1500 lofts in Melbourne, and that they all head directly for their own loft, then that's a pretty unique situation.

We have favourites, like in any sport, and the tendency is to favour the winners. But year in year out my favourite bird is the one that has a real go, the one that's in the first four every week.

RICHIE BENAUD

Part of my business activities take me to some strange places and, in order to write and talk about diets and food, I once did a cooking course in Italy.

It certainly boosted my knowledge of Italian food because it was run by the great chef Guiliano Bugiali, who didn't hang back when extolling the virtues or otherwise of the offerings served up by his pupils. And I learnt how to make my own pasta, beautifully fine in texture, but not all that easy to achieve.

In 97 Test innings Richie Benaud was never run out.

I was the risotto stirrer at the same time, and I can assure you stirring rice for 40 people is not recommended for those with weak muscles.

When Bugiali was doing the rounds, examining everyone's pasta, I was delighted that he spent so much time with the 30 x 60 centimetre sheet I had made as fine as tissue paper. I was prepared to hang on every word as he prodded and fondled the pasta, but he said nothing, so I tried to help.

"Any mistakes?" I asked genially.

"Quiet," he answered. "I was trying to count the mistakes, I'd reached seventeen and now I'll have to start again."

DAVID GOWER

Africa is a continent which I find fascinating, and the vastness and beauty of the great African bush is like a magnet to me. Having been brought up, at least until I was six, in what was then Tanganyika, now Tanzania, I have always had a strong affinity for wildlife—as opposed to wild life—and I now occupy some of my spare time by helping raise money for the conservation of Africa and its wildlife heritage.

Viewers of Channel Nine's cricket coverage over the last couple of seasons will have noticed my attempts to publicise the odd fundraiser I've hosted in Australia, under the auspices of the SAVE Foundation run by mate Nick Duncan in Perth. We have been concentrating our efforts on supporting the National Parks of Zimbabwe, where the biggest single problem is protecting the remaining few

David Gower twice scored 1000 Test runs in a calendar year; in 1982 (1061 at 46.13) and 1986 (1059 at 44.12).

hundred black rhino from the hands and guns of the poachers, who are effectively wiping out the rhino from that region.

The situation there is particularly dire, especially if you are a large, thick-skinned, horny mammal, naively thinking that you and your ancestors have been safe browsing around the bush for the last few million years, so that is what life is all about.

The battle is not exactly a fair contest, and rhino are being lost on an almost daily basis, despite all the efforts of those who are still trying to protect them.

I have hosted one safari to Zimbabwe, Zambia and Botswana under the SAVE banner—which left several thousand dollars in Harare for the cause—and also a couple of very successful nights, one at Coco's in Perth, one at

Doyle's in Sydney, which raised more than decent sums of money, thanks to some very generous bidders at the auctions.

If there was one principle guiding these events, it was that we had fun while remembering the reasons for being there. We were all helped by the likes of Rob and Judi Hirst, who brought the Bollinger that put everyone in the right mood to spend their money!

I might just mention that, after all our battles on the cricket field, for once I had Allan Border on my side as a supporter and friend, proving that the old boy does do something else apart from accumulate Test runs by the thousand. He doesn't turn down that Bollinger too often either!

IAN CHAPPELL

During my career playing cricket I played a lot of golf. I first started playing the game seriously on the tour of South Africa in 1966–67 and then continued playing it quite seriously during each winter.

I got my handicap down to seven at Glenelg golf club in Adelaide.

I always felt that golf was the perfect sport for cricketers. It got you out in the fresh air on a day off, and away from cricket and anybody who wanted to talk about the game.

It also didn't require too much energy when you had a couple of important days still to play in a Test.

When I retired from cricket and started working in television I realised that I was becoming a very inactive person after being a very active one. I thought this was dangerous, so I started playing tennis for exercise.

After a while I discovered I liked the game and it fulfilled

my competitive urge. I started out playing a lot of singles and still enjoy the one-on-one combat, as well as the exercise this brings.

However I've come to like doubles more and more as I unearth the intricacies of the game.

To improve my game I've played a few seasons of badge tennis in Sydney and I have an ambition to play in some veterans tournaments as time permits.

DAVID GOWER

Another little sideline that used to keep me amused in winters before I came out to join the Channel Nine cricket team was the noble art of tobogganing.

Mind you, I am not just talking about jumping on the traditional wooden sledge and bombing down any old hill, but about the serious stuff that happens down the Cresta Run, under the auspices of the St Moritz Tobogganing Club (SMTC).

The Cresta began, like most winter sports, with the 'Brits', who needed a course to hold races on, but it has now developed into a sport dominated more by the Europeans.

It is often confused with the Bob, which involves a two– or four–man sled making rapid progress down an ice run. The Cresta has you lying all alone on a low-slung 'skeleton' toboggan, going head first down the same sort of track, again at some speed.

My debut on the Cresta came a couple of weeks before my tour of the West Indies as captain in 1986. Allan Lamb was my competition on that trip, and some observers thought we were particularly irresponsible to be risking injury so soon before the tour.

They had a point, though we thought if we survived the Cresta we could look upon the West Indies fast bowlers with impunity. In the event, we survived the ice, but came off second best in the heat of the cauldron that is Test cricket

David Gower's bowling figures in the Second Test versus New Zealand at Trent Bridge, 1986, were unusual: 0–0–4–0. How could it be? Gower delivered one ball, but it was called a no-ball because the umpire ruled Gower's arm was suspiciously bent. The batsman Martin Crowe hit it for four. They were the winning runs, so Gower didn't have to bowl again.

in the Caribbean.

There are, it goes without saying, far better Cresta riders around than either myself or 'Lambie', but we do enjoy our own private battles on the run.

Last time we were there his chairman at Northamptonshire, Lynn Wilson, offered the prize of a suitable magnum of champagne to the winner, and the two of us entered in an official SMTC race.

As it happened, we arrived slightly too late to get our toboggans out of the clubhouse in time to qualify by the rules of racing. But for some reason the secretary of the club only spotted my opponent. The result was that, although Lambie actually rode the course quicker by about half a second, he was described on the official results as disqualified, leaving me the winner of the inaugural race for SMTC Test cricketers. Shame!

Sadly, there has yet to be a re-run, what with us being selected or not by England, or being selected instead by Nine, but there must come a time soon when we will both be free to continue that competition.

If nothing else, believe me, the Cresta is a very invigorating destination for a long weekend in the northern winter.

GREG CHAPPELL

One of the benefits of the cricket era in which I played was that we had to have a career outside the game. In other words, when cricket was over we had a job or a business to continue with.

We didn't have the worries of today's players—finishing with cricket, then looking around and trying to decide what we'd do. During my cricket days I was involved in the insurance industry, but there was also a phase when I was

> *With the cover photo for a book in mind Greg Chappell set an extraordinary field during a Test against New Zealand at Christchurch in 1977. When Dennis Lillee bowled it was to nine slips!*

in public relations and promotions with the Coca-Cola Bottling Company in Adelaide.

When I moved to Queensland I went back into the insurance industry because it gave me the chance to earn as much in the months between cricket as I could have earned at any other job working fulltime, provided I worked hard enough at it.

We had our own business in Queensland called Living Insurance, which was to the life insurance industry what Kerry Packer's World Series Cricket was to cricket—a bit of a revolution in its own right.

That's to say it was a very different insurance product from that which was already available.

These days I'm involved in another 'revolution'—this time in the golfing world with a company called Fundamental Golf and Leisure Ltd., which owns 49 percent of Fundamental Golf, a company owned by Gerry Hogan, Michael Hammond, Bob Barraket and me.

We promote a particular golf club shaft technology that has been developed by Gerry Hogan here in Australia.

And we manufacture and market our own brand of golf clubs: The Fundamental 21 AD range, as in the 21st century *ano domini*. In other words, we believe it is the technology for the 21st century.

We are also licensing the technology to other manufacturers and we receive a royalty for that, particularly with the shaft as it is all 'patent pending' at the moment.

Nobody can use the technology unless they get a licence from us. We also have the option to licence the selling of our own range of clubs, and we are looking to do that in

America and Japan, Europe and South-east Asia.

The irony of my close business involvement in golf will not be lost on many of my old cricketing friends, because there was a time when I wasn't nearly as keen on the game as they were.

Golf is probably the most difficult game because it is proactive, whereas the other sports I played, cricket or baseball, are re-active. In those sports you have to react to what the bowler or pitcher has done, and you are relying basically on your reflexes and your experience over years and years.

In golf, you have the ball sitting there and you have to create the action. As well as that you have a lot more time to think about what you are doing, conscious thinking that can interfere with what you want to do.

In cricket there is very little time for conscious thought. Once the ball has been bowled you really don't have time to consider your technique, you just react by instinct.

My theory about golf is that you should treat it like cricket and not stand over the ball thinking too long, otherwise you could make the game more difficult.

In my cricketing days I got into golf more or less as a result of the adage "If you can't beat 'em, join 'em". Fellows like Rod Marsh used to go out every rest day during Tests and play golf, and when they returned to the bar they would replay every shot, shot for shot.

I couldn't believe they could spend all day playing the game and all night talking about it. Anyway I decided there must be something in it, so I joined them. It was enjoyable relaxation to get out in the open air rather than hang about the team hotel.

I found it interesting that when I did start to play I was determined to win. In other words you can take somebody who is quite competitive in one sport and put them in another sport where they'll be equally competitive. The person's level of skill at the other game might not be as high, but the competitive drive remains just as intense. Doug Walters was a good example.

As with his cricket his style was quite unique, only more so. He played golf both hands, getting to the green via shots played with a right-handed stance, but then putted left-handed. At one stage he was putting with his left hand down near the blade and his right hand at the top of the putter.

Basically he was crouched over, shovelling the ball into the hole, but let me assure you, off his quite liberal handicap he was quite a competitor.

Rod Marsh was probably the best of the golfing cricketers of my era, but since then I have seen Allan Border, Mark and Peter Taylor, who are all very good golfers.

Steve Waugh and Jeff Thomson probably have the best natural golf hitting styles of any cricketers I have played with. They hit the ball very much like the professionals, although sometimes not in the desired direction! But they have style, and great 'hands', and hit the ball a long way.

Golf took my mind off cricket and the problems it entailed. Over a period of some years golf was very therapeutic; through the tough eighties and early nineties golf helped me pull through.

Now I have been able to make it a business. It was a great challenge, because this technology of ours flew in the face of conventional wisdom. But all the tests have proved that Gerry Hogan is correct, and this may well be the golf technology for the 21st century.

It is the most challenging and exciting thing I have been involved in since World Series Cricket; the fact that it was developed in Australia, and the thought that we are taking it to the rest of the world, really excites me.

Chapter Ten

Night Tests?
God Forbid!

In 1977 the sun set on the cricket traditionalists' theory that the great game could only be played in God's daylight and with a red ball. By the light of the moon cricket attracted a new and vibrant audience.

Night cricket was the innovation that set breakaway World Series Cricket, and what was called 'official cricket', apart. Its success not only ensured the two factions would one day be reunited for the good of the game, but it ensured the game would move into a more popular format.

The future success of night cricket was guaranteed on November 28, 1978, when ground authorities had to throw open—not close—the gates at the SCG for a limited-overs World Series Cricket match between Australia and the West Indies.

Gatemen simply couldn't cope with the queues stretching away from the entrance gates, and feared any delay in allowing them to enter might cause panic, with terrible consequences.

The attendance was estimated at 50,000. Richie Benaud still says, "I have never before or after seen, or felt, anything to match it."

The question is: does that mean the same thing would happen if a Test match was to be played at night?

IAN CHAPPELL

Night Tests? As New South Wales Liberal premier John Fahey said about Australia becoming a republic, "It's inevitable."

The only stumbling blocks are finding a white ball that will go the distance and the fact that not all grounds have lights of sufficient standard to stage a Test.

The first problem can surely be overcome with the advances in modern technology. The second point shouldn't be an obstacle: I don't see why one country should be penalised because others haven't upgraded, or can't afford to upgrade their facilities.

Night Tests would enable people to watch a good portion of a day's play without missing work and it would be a godsend for players who have skin cancer problems.

GREG CHAPPELL

Test cricket at night is an option that must be seriously explored. The problem with night cricket is the change from daylight to dark. Most times in Australia conditions are pretty good with bright sunny days, but obviously the light changes during that transition period when the artificial light chimes in and takes over from the natural light.

If you can organise your break periods, dinner breaks and so on to coincide with that time you can overcome part of the problem. The other problem of course is with balls. Currently the only ball you can use under night conditions is the white ball.

So then you have to decide whether you are going to use the white ball for daytime cricket, because you can't have a situation where you are using the red ball through the day and a white ball during the night. Another problem to deal with is whether all grounds are going to have lights, or whether you are going to have only some Test matches played under lights.

There is one argument that one-day cricket and Test cricket should be separated, and one good way of separating them is to have limited-overs cricket played under lights, and Test matches played during the day. I don't fully agree with that. I believe that the option should be there to play Test cricket under lights. I think it's another move into the 21st century.

It's going to be a matter of public demand: if they are going to continue to watch Test cricket, one of the ways they will watch more of it is to have it at night.

If you can sort out those negative aspects of the changed conditions both in light and the ball, then I think Test cricket should move towards day/night cricket.

TONY GREIG

As far as Test cricket at night is concerned, I would be inclined to leave things as they are. Cricket in Australia has found a healthy mix between the traditional five-day Test format and the limited-overs game. On average we play 25 days of Test cricket and 15 one-day Internationals.

To try to mix into Test cricket some of the successes of one-day cricket would detract from both formats. Test cricket in coloured clothing under lights is a little too much just now. I've always looked on one-day cricket as 'fast food', while Tests retain the qualities associated with fine food.

Hopefully the youngsters that the marketing of one-day cricket attracts will turn into lovers of the traditional game. After all, if fast food and French restaurants can co-exist, I see no reason why limited-overs and Tests cannot do the same.

BILL LAWRY

I don't believe that Test cricket should be played at night. It will be confusing the game with the one-day Internationals.

I also believe that Test cricket is unique. It is a game that starts at 11 a.m. and finishes at 6 p.m., played in creams and with a red ball. I believe that if administrators worldwide decide to take cricket into the night we'll certainly lose out comparatively to the hurly-burly of the one-day game in which people expect to get plenty of action, especially in the final session of an evening.

One other consideration is the television side of things. Night Tests might not receive the same extensive cover as day Tests do today.

Chapter Eleven

Muddles in
the Middle

*Life has suddenly become a handful for cricket's umpires;
what was once the relatively simple task of either giving
a player the benefit of the doubt, or giving another the
benefit of a raised index finger, is these days a much
more complicated business.*

*Defining a bumper used to be simple, now there is a
hint that in his pocket, as well as chewing gum, scissors
and tape, an umpire might find a theodolite useful.*

*Human error used to be a useful ally for an umpire,
but now the television replay has given human error a
new meaning. And more than that, visiting players from
other countries are linking bias to an umpire's
birthplace.*

*Words like "neutral" are being mentioned in cricket
reports, whereas once it was a word reserved for war
reports and how-to-drive-a-car manuals.*

*And "neutral" may not be the only aspect of motoring
to infiltrate the great game. If a third umpire assisted by
a television video is introduced then a batsman may get
'the green light'—if he is lucky.*

*If there is green there must be red. Will there be an
amber, the 'on hold' light in case the third umpire's
deliberations hit the wall, however momentarily?*

Shades of a traffic jam at the corner of Market and Pitt!

In 1993—the year of the television replay umpire—in New Zealand during a limited-overs International, Pakistan's Shahid Saeed was adjudged run out via the TV replay umpire, after a direct hit.

The replay showed that Saeed's bat was on the line ... yes, on the line is out, no doubt about that. Close, but according to the rules, out!

This prompted the Pakistan manager, Naushad Ali, to call for batsmen to be given the benefit of the doubt in especially close situations, even when the TV replay is in use.

The first question is: how far "out" is "especially close"? The next question is: why should "out" be "not out"? Finally why, if it's preferable to retain the old 'benefit of the doubt' philosophy, do we have to introduce umpiring by TV replays?

Does cricket really need a television umpire? Does it really need so-called neutral umpires?

IAN CHAPPELL

Umpires are already neutral.

Suggestions about having neutral umpires, an international panel, a third umpire and video replays ignore the problems. The standard of umpiring needs to be improved and the acceptance of umpires' decisions by players leaves a lot to be desired.

Every effort should be made to solve these problems, because if successful, it would alleviate the need to change the system drastically.

If the measures I suggest fail, I would opt for an umpire

from each participating country to stand in every international match as the next best solution.

I accept television replays as the third umpire in limited-overs Internationals, but not in Tests. The one-day game is entertainment, while a Test match should be entertainment, plus a true test of each player's worth.

If you only have replays available for some decisions and not others, then in effect you're saying one batsman's wicket is more valuable than that of another. The wicket of every batsman should be of equal importance.

I've never heard of a player whose career was wrecked by a solitary bad decision. If you're good enough to play a lengthy career then the good and bad decisions even out. And if the standard of umpiring is improved, there'll be less bad ones and more good ones.

To bring in a *proper* television replay system, separate from the actual television coverage and with appropriate cameras and video machines, is a costly exercise—around $5000 a day. If that sort of money is available then why aren't umpires better paid?

At those sort of rates and with the option to fast track former first-class players into the system, the standard of umpiring could be improved very quickly.

If fewer and fewer players have a job during their cricket career because of the time off required, then presumably they'll find it difficult to get a job when they retire.

If umpiring is made more attractive, then surely more ex-players would be candidates for the job.

Let's say nothing is done and the video replay is universally adopted. What will happen when an umpire calls for help in front of a huge crowd and the reply comes back, "Sorry the tape's ruined and we can't help you"?

Then the umpire, who has already indicated to the masses that he doesn't know the answer, still has to give a decision. Good luck if he rules against the home side.

The human element in umpiring and preparation of pitches is vital to Test cricket. It should always be remembered that what we are talking about is a *game*, not something that saves or costs lives.

If you want robot umpires that never err, then why not computerised players who never make a mistake?

If you want robot umpires and pitches that never vary, then go ahead and bring in television replays and artificial pitches. But for God's sake don't call it a Test and don't ask me to watch.

TONY GREIG

The concept of neutral umpires has been debated for some time and has been introduced in some countries. Most followers of the game are happy to concede that some countries would benefit in the short term by the introduction of neutral umpires in Test matches. But the overall object should be to raise the standard of umpires at all levels of cricket worldwide on an ongoing basis.

To do this, Test umpires have to be underpinned by State and club umpires, who themselves must have a ladder to climb, the ultimate rung of which is to stand in a Test match.

English umpires start by playing club cricket and then go on to make a career in County cricket, and in some cases become Test match umpires. Imagine if they were told that umpires from a neutral country would be standing in their place in Test matches in England—they would justifiably feel hard done by.

English umpires are, after all, better umpires than most, largely because most of them have played first-class cricket. The umpires in all the other countries around the world are definitely not as good as their English colleagues, and therefore a case does exist to create a panel who would stand in big matches around the world.

Alternatively umpiring has to be made attractive to former first-class cricketers worldwide.

Pakistan, whose umpires are constantly criticised, are in favour of neutral umpires, because the crowds and players place extra pressure on their umpires in home Tests.

Bill Lawry tells me South Africa would never agree to neutral umpires, because if they did they would never win! Coming from an Aussie who was never, not even once, given out leg before in a Test in Australia is a bit rich, but then again he never got hit on the pads—so he says! So the argument goes on.

Before one considers any changes, the substantial costs of having neutral umpires needs to be investigated, because it may be that cricket in some countries can't afford the outlay. My feeling is that each country should make its own decision and pay its own costs.

I am totally in favour of replays being used to aid the umpire. After all, the umpires of yesteryear never had to confront the problems associated with television replays, or hostile commentators who all have the benefit of video replays. As a result their decisions were always a matter of opinion, but never proved one way or the other. Now decisions are made that are proved beyond doubt to be good or bad.

The average cricket lover is no fool—if a batsman is out the viewer in the loungeroom has a pretty good idea once the replay has been shown, and in my capacity as a commentator I am not prepared to make too many excuses

---

The Indian spinner Bishen Bedi's 200th Test victim was Tony Greig, caught Viswanath in the Third Test at Madras, 1976–77.

for bad umpires. Because replays are being used as a vehicle to criticise the umpires, why not give the umpires the very instrument that is making the job so hard?

Let's face it, a top umpire won't call for help too often and when he does he will be making that decision in the name of getting the decision right, and that is good for the game.

It's a pretty weak state of affairs when a close run-out which could decide the outcome of a match is replayed and the umpire is made to look stupid.

Allow the umpire to decide when he needs help. He would then call in the third umpire, who is required to be on the ground, to view the replay and indicate 'out', 'not out' or 'too close to call'.

All the International Cricket Conference has to do is come up with a standard format on what colour light should be used to indicate if a batsman is out or not. Logic would suggest red for 'out', green for 'not out' and orange for 'too close to call' or 'not conclusive'.

BILL LAWRY

The umpiring problem is a great concern to all who love the game of cricket, or play it, or indeed administer it. A top quality match needs top quality umpires.

While players have been given every opportunity to advance their skills, particularly in modern times, players worldwide have treated umpires like second-class citizens.

It gets back to the local competitions—they need to put as much effort into the training and encouragement of umpires as they do with players. Unless all countries improve the standard of umpiring at first-class level, it won't matter whether neutral umpires or home umpires are used,

YOU'D BETTER USE THE GREEN TO SIGNAL 'OUT' — HE WON'T WALK AGAINST A RED LIGHT...!

and the controversies that seem to appear because of umpires' decisions will continue.

The use of television replays for run-outs in one-day Internationals and Test matches will certainly take some of the pressure off modern umpires. Umpires in previous generations did not have to face the repeated television replays, in slow motion, of each decision they made. Umpires these days do, and it does put them under a lot more pressure than their counterparts of yesteryear. But neutral umpires will not stop the controversy. The mistake will still be shown on television; the fact will remain, the umpires are not of top quality.

A television umpire certainly was successful in New Zealand when Australia toured in 1993. Eventually it will be used, I would suggest, in most countries in one-day Internationals where there seem to be a lot more run-outs as a result of desperation to try to score off every ball.

It does take a lot of pressure off the two umpires when run-out decisions are adjudicated by a third umpire and a television—and I think that is important. If cricket can afford to have television cameras and the third umpire at the grounds for one-day Internationals, I think it should be encouraged. All the talk after New Zealand was that the replays and the third umpire not only gave the batsmen and the fielding side fair decisions, but also really brought the spectators into play. It was all over very quickly and of course, the roar or the groan went up depending on what the final result was from the third umpire.

So I can imagine that when used with the big screen the third umpire decisions in one-day Internationals will be a major contributor to the entertainment of the crowd. And that, after all, is what one-day cricket is all about—players showing their attacking skills and entertaining the masses who, by coming along, are the financial support of cricket in general.

I'm not quite sure whether the television umpire is warranted, or needed, in Test matches, though. That is something for administrators to decide in the future. Certainly I think the one thing it would do is take the pressure off the umpires by removing a lot of the controversy in run-out decisions. For some reason umpires seem to be getting them wrong on a fair number of occasions.

GREG CHAPPELL

I'm comfortable with the current system, where you have the third umpire in place in limited-overs matches for run-outs and stumpings, and I don't see that it should necessarily be just left in the domain of one-day cricket.

It won't mean that you'll rule out all errors. There are going to be times when it's too close to call and the benefit of doubt must go to the batsman.

From my experience sitting in the commentary position and watching replays of run-outs, stumpings and other incidents, there have been times where the commentary panel is equally divided after watching replay after replay as to whether it was out or it wasn't out.

So there are going to be times when the third umpire is put under just as much pressure as an umpire in the middle.

And again I say, as long as the benefit of doubt goes towards the batsman, I don't see a problem.

However, I can't see how the third umpire on the television replay is going to be of much value outside of run-outs and stumpings.

DAVID GOWER

Apart from vague calls to uphold the traditions of the game, the only objection I hear nowadays to the use of television umpires is that technology cannot as yet cope with the many other contentious decisions that the poor old umpire has to make, bat and pad chances and the like, and as such the system remains unfair.

I say that anything which helps umpires reach the correct decision must be a step in the right direction, given that even television is not infallible, with players often getting in the way, obscuring the view just at the crucial moment. Co-operation between cricket's authorities and television's producers is also essential, remembering that television's first reason for being present is not to adjudicate on run-outs. An understanding must be reached on efficient working arrangements that will not push the costs too high.

The good news is that crowds seem to love the suspense generated by referring the case to the third umpire (while the batsman sweats it out until the decision is handed down from the high court) and no more will the umpire have to endure the castigation of us commentators with all that technology at our disposal to prove his eyes once again fallible.

Umpires must of course maintain the high standards universally expected of players and officials in every sport, and it is only fair to hope that the best umpires will be available as often as possible around the world. I am not sure that we need so-called neutral officials in every series, as that will not solve all the problems at stake, but I am happy that moves are happening to make the option possible around the world.

If boards wish to consult and discuss the option before every series, they can then take the option to employ neutrals if required. But, at the risk of sounding blindly patriotic, I would be very reluctant to see English umpires replaced by overseas neutrals, especially if it was apparent that the neutrals did not match up to the expected high standards.

All that said, I have seen top-class umpires at work in almost every Test-playing country. Umpires with the least experience are understandably the ones prone to making more mistakes. Nobody becomes proficient in any activity overnight, but as long as everyone is striving to attain high standards, the situation should gradually improve worldwide, especially if continued steps are taken to make the umpire's job less, not more, complicated.

One point worth making is that the overall health of the game remains the responsibility of the captains and players. Entertainment is still of paramount importance, which puts the onus on the players to be positive in their outlook and approach to the game. Thankfully this seems to be happening: last summer's Australia versus West Indies series saw some great cricket from both sides, and England's problems in India all stemmed from the brilliance of Mohammed Azharuddin on the first day of the series in Calcutta. His innings set the tone for the Indian batsmen to follow through the series, and nobody could accuse them of dull cricket.

Chapter Twelve

The Favoured Few

"There's music in the names I used to know,
And magic when I heard them, long ago ..."

THE NAMES, BY THOMAS MOULT

Naming favourite players is a favourite pastime. Some
are inspired by the most recent events on the field, others
retain fondest memories of those players with whom they
took the field.

RICHIE BENAUD

Keith Miller, Arthur Morris and Ray Lindwall were the three
players who had the most beneficial effect on my career for
New South Wales and Australia. Miller was the best
allrounder I ever played with or against and a brilliant
captain.

> *When England needed 97 in their second innings to*
> *win the Fourth Test—and win back the Ashes—against*
> *Australia at Adelaide in 1954–55, Keith Miller, before*
> *he took the field, said, "Somebody's in for a nasty*
> *half-hour." He got rid of Hutton, Bill Edrich and*
> *Cowdrey in 20 balls, but then damaged his shoulder*
> *taking a smart catch to dismiss May. England won by*
> *five wickets.*

He taught me how to stay two overs ahead of the game, to try to keep the opposition on the wrong foot and not to fear being unorthodox. He was a wonderful player and a great personality.

IAN CHAPPELL

Doug Walters. Anyone who has the ability to score a Test hundred in a session three times is a great player. Doug is also endowed with a comedian's good timing. I said I'd hate to play in an Australian team without Walters and fortunately it didn't happen often.

BILL LAWRY

Richie Richardson, the West Indian captain, is my favourite player mainly because he is one of the few batsmen in the world today who can turn a match in a session, or even an hour's play.

He's also one of the few top-order batsmen who are prepared to take the attack to genuine fast bowlers, without wearing a helmet. Indeed, last season in Australia his big red hat became one of the features of the Australian summer, as did his attacking batting, whether his side was in trouble or forging towards a victory.

TONY GREIG

Gary Sobers, later Sir Garfield, is by far my favourite cricketer. I cannot think of anyone with such an elevated sporting profile who possesses so many great qualities. I was lucky enough to tour Australia under 'Sobie'. He was the captain of the World XI, which consisted of a cross-section

> *Gary Sobers hit 10 fours in an innings of 43 against Australia at Bridgetown, Barbados, 1955.*

of South Africans, Pakistanis, Indians, New Zealanders and Englishmen.

To watch him bat, bowl and field was cricket poetry in motion. To be part of his everyday cricketing routine for a few months of his life was a privilege.

It was inspiring to experience first-hand his refreshing and positive approach to every aspect of the game. As a man and friend he is totally honest, open and absolutely genuine.

He takes, but more importantly gives, and he understands and implements that all-important requirement in life, two-way traffic.

Cricket has never had a greater ambassador.

GREG CHAPPELL

My favourite cricketer, as far as watching someone play, was *Dennis Lillee*. Dennis in his early days was a tearaway, young fast bowler who had to rebuild his body as well as his action after his serious back injury.

Of all the bowlers I played with or against I enjoyed watching Dennis in action the most—even when I was batting against him! True, that was a difficult exercise, because he made a batsman think more than any other bowler I ever saw.

His attributes were his variety, his consistency, his big

> *Dennis Lillee broke the world record for wickets when West Indian Larry Gomes became his 311th Test victim, caught Greg Chappell, at the MCG in the 1981–82 season.*

heart and his ability to build himself up for the big effort, particularly when conditions didn't suit him.

As an example, on the tour to Pakistan in 1980, where they made the pitches low and slow to blunt Dennis' bowling, at no stage did he give up.

He gave 150 percent effort, never once complained and just got on with doing the best he could.

DAVID GOWER

My hope is that the game will continue to throw up the players to entertain future generations. And with that principle of spirit and entertainment in mind, I can only nominate *Ian Botham*. I cannot agree with everything my old mate has either said or done, but I can only admire the

THEY CAN SAY WHAT THEY LIKE ABOUT HIM – HE'S ALWAYS ENTERTAINING!

> *In the 1985 Edgbaston Test against Australia Ian Botham came to bat with England 4/572. He hit the first ball he received from fast bowler Craig McDermott down the ground for six—one of 80 sixes he hit that summer, and a record. The previous best was by another Somerset player, Arthur Wellard, 66 in 1935.*

qualities he did bring to international cricket. Foremost among these were the belief that he could do anything on a cricket field. We all know that even 'Both' had human limitations, but he did stretch them amazingly at times, as more than one Australian side found out.

For all his talent, it will be for his bravado and for living the game and life to the full that I will remember Ian; and just the memories of trying to keep up with the man leaves me feeling weary!

WHY THE TEAM MADE THEM FAVOURITES

Keith Ross Miller saw duty in World War II as a fighter pilot, then made his Test debut in the very first Test match after the war, Australia against New Zealand at Basin Reserve, when the Kiwis succumbed to Bill O'Reilly and Ernie Toshack on a rain-affected pitch, making only 42 and 54.

Miller made 30 runs and only bowled six overs; his first series against England in 1946–47 was a memorable one. In the First Test in Brisbane he made 79 and took 7/60, which was to remain his best bowling in Tests.

In the series, he finished second in the batting to Bradman (384 runs at 76.80) and second in the bowling behind Lindwall (16 wickets at 20.87), although it was possibly of little concern to Miller, for he maintained a wonderfully casual approach to the game. Success could depend on his mood. On the 1948 tour to England when Australia scored 700 in a day against Essex, Miller allowed himself to be bowled for a 'duck', evidence many believed of his sportsmanlike attitude to the game. Yet, seven times in his career he scored more than 200 runs in an innings.

Miller was a crowd-pleaser, standing over six feet (180 centimetres), magnificently athletic and with a mane of long, black hair that flew into his face in moments of action, but was flicked back with a majestic toss of the head.

He was a stroke-playing batsman, favouring the 'long handle' approach; his bowling action was classically high, and at times he could be faster than Lindwall.

In today's world of whiz-bang limited-overs cricket he would have been a sensation!

Test Career of Miller, K R

Batting

Opponents	Debut	M	Inn	N.O	Runs	H.S	50	100	Avrge
England	1946/47	29	49	4	1511	*145	6	3	33.58
India	1947/48	5	5	–	185	67	2	–	37.00
New Zealand	1945/46	1	1	–	30	30	–	–	30.00
Pakistan	1956/57	1	2	–	32	21	–	–	16.00
South Africa	1949/50	9	14	2	399	84	4	–	33.25
West Indies	1951/52	10	16	1	801	147	1	4	53.40
Total		55	87	7	2958	147	13	7	36.98

Bowling

Opponents	Debut	M	Ball	Mdns	Runs	Wkts	Avrge	5	Best	Stk/Rt	RPO	Eco/Rt
England	1946/47	29	5645	225	1949	87	22.40	3	7/60	64.89	2.07	34.53
India	1947/48	5	576	14	223	9	24.78	–	2/25	64.00	2.32	38.72
New Zealand	1945/46	1	36	2	6	2	3.00	–	2/6	18.00	1.00	16.67
Pakistan	1956/57	1	174	9	58	2	29.00	–	2/40	87.00	2.00	33.33
South Africa	1949/50	9	1801	34	631	30	21.03	1	5/40	60.03	2.10	35.04
West Indies	1951/52	10	2157	53	1039	40	25.98	3	6/107	53.93	2.89	48.17
Total		55	10389	337	3906	170	22.98	7	7/60	61.11	2.26	37.60

Richie Benjamin Richardson was born in Antigua in the Caribbean, the home of that other great West Indian batsman, an 'almost namesake', Richards, Isaac Vivian Alexander. A remarkable double for such a tiny island.

Not only that, he took over the captaincy from Richards and, leading from the front by way of his batting blitzes and a cool head in any moment of crisis, he has managed to keep his team at the head of the Test playing nations, despite the West Indies being in somewhat of a rebuilding stage.

His rarely-heard nickname is 'Bubbler', and that might provide the clue to this success against the odds: the cricket is never dull when Richardson is the centrepiece of the action.

He made his first tour for the West Indies at 21, to India, yet he had only made his inter-island Shield debut a year before, because soccer had been his game.

He made his mark in the last three Tests against Kim Hughes' team in the Caribbean in 1984, scoring two centuries, and has never looked back.

When the Australians seemed to be getting on top early in the 1991 tour it was Richardson's extraordinary free-hitting 182 that broke the spirit of Border's men and proved to be the turning point of the series.

In fact it is Australia for whom Richardson reserves his very best.

Test Career of Richardson, R B

Batting

Opponents	Debut	M	Inn	N.O	Runs	H.S	50	100	Avrge
Australia	1983/84	25	40	3	1946	182	7	8	52.59
England	1985/86	17	30	3	1148	160	3	4	42.52
India	1983/84	9	17	2	871	194	5	2	58.07
New Zealand	1984/85	7	11	1	512	185	2	1	51.20
Pakistan	1986/87	9	17	1	550	75	4	–	34.38
South Africa	1991/92	1	2	–	46	44	–	-	23.00
Total		68	117	10	5073	194	21	15	47.41

Gary St Aubrun Sobers was 17 years and 245 days when he made his Test debut in the final Test against England at Kingston, Jamaica in 1954. He took 4/75. It was at Kingston four years later against Pakistan that he scored 365 not out, thus eclipsing the previous highest score in Test cricket, 364 by Sir Len Hutton, which had stood since 1938.

Sobers batted for a tick over 10 hours, three less than Hutton. He hit 38 boundaries, and it was his first three-figure score in Tests.

In that series Sobers, only 21 years old, made 824 runs; he was to aggregate 500 runs in five other Test series in his career. At one stage he played 85 consecutive Tests.

One of his greatest innings was his 254 for the Rest Of The World against Australia at the MCG in 1971–72. Those who saw it rated it among the most masterly ever played.

Playing for Nottingham against Glamorgan in 1968 he hit the left-arm orthodox spinner Malcolm Nash for six consecutive sixes.

In 1975 in Barbados, his birthplace, he was knighted by the Queen for his services to cricket.

Test Career of Sobers, G S

Batting

Opponents	Debut	M	Inn	N.O	Runs	H.S	50	100	Avrge
Australia	1954/55	19	38	3	1510	168	6	4	43.14
England	1953/54	36	61	8	3214	226	13	10	60.64
India	1958/59	18	30	7	1920	198	7	8	83.48
New Zealand	1955/56	12	18	1	404	142	–	1	23.76
Pakistan	1957/58	8	13	2	984	*365	4	3	89.45
Total		93	160	21	8032	*365	30	26	57.78

Bowling

Opponents	Debut	M	Ball	Mdns	Runs	Wkts	Avrge	5	Best	Stk/Rt	RPO	Eco/Rt
Australia	1954/55	19	4895	154	2024	51	39.69	2	6/73	95.98	2.48	41.35
England	1953/54	36	8771	411	3323	102	32.58	3	5/41	85.99	2.27	37.89

Bowling (*cont.*)

India	1958/59	18	4301	215	1516	59	25.69	1	5/63	72.90	2.11	35.25
New Zealand	1955/56	12	2207	105	682	19	35.89	–	4/64	116.16	1.85	30.90
Pakistan	1957/58	8	1425	89	454	4	113.50	–	2/41	356.25	1.91	31.86
Total		93	21599	974	7999	235	34.04	6	6/73	91.91	2.22	37.03

Dennis Keith Lillee took 5/84 on his Test debut in Adelaide, against Ray Illingworth's 1970–71 touring team, which won back the Ashes. It was during this series that Bill Lawry was sacked and Ian Chappell took over, eventually leading the

1972 team back to England.

Lillee was on that tour, and although Australia couldn't lift the Ashes Lillee took a record 31 wickets in the series, and took 10 wickets in the final Test victory at the Oval which enabled Australia to at least draw the series.

In the very next series, against Pakistan in Australia, Lillee's back problems began and he broke down badly during the 1973 tour to the West Indies.

He hardly bowled a ball in anger for two seasons, opting instead for a special medical programme devised to strengthen his back, and he worked on improving his batting.

That was to save Australia's bacon in the Lord's Test in 1975 when, with the team 8/133 in reply to England's 315, Lillee scored an unbeaten 73.

Like all fast bowlers aggression was never far from the surface, although in Lillee's case it may have bubbled over once or twice, most obviously in the Miandad incident and the aluminium bat incident, both in his home town Perth.

Strangely enough it is two bowling performances in one-off Tests that still most capture people's imagination.

Against the Rest Of The World in 1970 in Perth he took 8/29 in only 7.1 overs, and then at the MCG in the Centenary Test he took 6/26 and 5/139, more or less ensuring an historic victory for Australia.

Test Career of Lillee, D K

Batting

Opponents	Debut	M	Inn	N.O	Runs	H.S	50	100	Avrge
England	1970/71	29	39	13	469	*73	1	–	18.04
India	1980/81	3	5	1	40	19	–	–	10.00
New Zealand	1976/77	8	9	1	130	27	–	–	16.25
Pakistan	1972/73	17	21	6	153	27	–	–	10.20
Sri Lanka	1982/83	1	–	–	–	–	–	–	–
West Indies	1972/73	12	16	3	113	25	–	–	8.69
Total		70	90	24	905	*73	1	–	13.71

Bowling

Opponents	Debut	M	Ball	Mdns	Runs	Wkts	Avrge	5	Best	Stk/Rt	RPO	Eco/Rt
England	1970/71	29	8516	361	3507	167	21.00	11	7/89	50.99	2.47	41.18
India	1980/81	3	891	33	452	21	21.52	–	4/65	42.43	3.04	50.73
New Zealand	1976/77	8	1770	63	740	38	19.47	4	6/53	46.58	2.51	41.81
Pakistan	1972/73	17	4433	127	2161	71	30.44	5	6/82	62.44	2.92	48.75
Sri Lanka	1982/83	1	180	6	107	3	35.67	–	2/67	60.00	3.57	59.44
West Indies	1972/73	12	2677	62	1526	55	27.75	3	7/83	48.67	3.42	57.00
Total		70	18467	652	8493	355	23.92	23	7/83	52.02	2.76	45.99

Ian Terence Botham The legend was born in the quarter final of an English Benson and Hedges Cup match between his team, Somerset, and Hampshire back in 1974. He was 18 years old. Hampshire had made 182, in which Botham had bowled the great Barry Richards for 13.

When Botham came to bat Somerset were 7/113, and soon eight out for 133, the destroyer being Hampshire's imported fast bowler, the very fast West Indian Andy Roberts.

When the total reached 131 Botham hooked at a bumper from Roberts, missed and was hit in the mouth, losing two teeth and a fair amount of blood.

But he batted on to crack the winning boundary with just one over to spare. The crowd invaded the pitch to salute him and the next morning he was headline news on every sports page in the country.

He played his first Test against Australia when he was just 21 years old, and took 5/21 at Trent Bridge. It was to be the forerunner of much success against the old enemy, much of it in improbable circumstances.

So much so that many believed he had a hex on the Australians. The most notable evidence of that was during the 1981 Ashes series in England when Botham, after resigning the captaincy following the Lord's Test, turned the series England's way with the most extraordinary personal performances.

At Headingley he hit a century off only 87 balls, his eventual 149 setting up an "impossible" England victory; later in the series he sealed another extraordinary England win by taking five wickets for one run in only 28 balls.

Even in his declining moments he turned a World Cup game against Australia, when he instigated a middle-order collapse at the SCG in 1992. He said he had done it for the Queen—the great Australian republic debate was getting underway at the time!

It was a comment that perfectly summed up the bigness of Botham.

Test Career of Botham, I T

Batting

Opponents	Debut	M	Inn	N.O	Runs	H.S	50	100	Avrge
Australia	1977	36	59	2	1673	*149	6	4	29.35
India	1979	14	17	–	1201	208	5	5	70.65
New Zealand	1977/78	15	23	2	846	138	4	3	40.29
Pakistan	1978	14	21	1	647	108	3	2	32.35
Sri Lanka	1981/82	3	3	–	41	22	–	–	13.67
West Indies	1980	20	38	1	792	81	4	–	21.41
Total		102	161	6	5200	208	22	14	33.55

Bowling

Opponents	Debut	M	Ball	Mdns	Runs	Wkts	Avrge	5	Best	Stk/Rt	RPO	Eco/Rt
Australia	1977	36	8479	297	4093	148	27.66	9	6/78	57.29	2.90	48.27
India	1979	14	3371	131	1558	59	26.41	6	7/48	57.14	2.77	46.22
New Zealand	1977/78	15	3284	120	1500	64	23.44	6	6/34	51.31	2.74	45.68
Pakistan	1978	14	2491	95	1271	40	31.78	2	8/34	62.28	3.06	51.02
Sri Lanka	1981/82	3	581	19	310	11	28.18	1	6/90	52.82	3.20	53.36
West Indies	1980	20	3609	126	2146	61	35.18	3	8/103	59.16	3.57	59.46
Total		102	21815	788	10878	383	28.40	27	8.34	56.96	2.99	49.86

Kevin Douglas Walters, Doug to everyone, came from the New South Wales dairy town of Dungog. He was just a teenager when he was spotted by the NSW selector Jack Chegwyn, who enjoyed taking teams of internationals to the country where they played against local teams.

Walters went to Sydney, where he played with Richie Benaud's club, Central Cumberland, now Parramatta. It wasn't long before crowds were calling him 'Dashing Doug' and he was only 20 years old when he played his first Test, against England at the Gabba in 1965. He scored 155 on debut, and the two shots that made the greatest number of runs for him, the pull and the cover drive, were in clear evidence then.

Yet his career faltered almost immediately when he was drafted into National Service (the Vietnam war) and Test

crowds didn't see him again until the Australians toured
England in 1968.

England, with its seaming wickets, was never really a
happy run hunting ground for Walters, nor was South Africa,
although he did run into John Snow and Mike Procter when
they were at their most lethal, each choosing to relentlessly

pound away with short balls around the off stump, or at him.

Walters was a magnificent player of spin, always prepared to use his feet to dance down the pitch and drive, often with his unique 'come to attention' style, where he would slide his back foot up to the front just as he made contact.

In 1968–69, against the West Indies at the SCG, he hit 242 and 103 to make him the first batsman to score a double-century and a century in the same Test. Eight years later he scored his second Test double-century, 250 against New Zealand in Christchurch.

In 1974–75, against England at Perth, he hit an unbeaten century in a session, tea to stumps, and got there with a pulled six off the last ball of the day! He remains one of Australia's most popular sportsmen.

Test Career of Walters, K D

Batting

Opponents	Debut	M	Inn	N.O	Runs	H.S	50	100	Avrge
England	1965/66	37	62	6	1981	155	13	4	35.38
India	1967/68	10	17	5	756	102	7	1	63.00
New Zealand	1973/74	11	16	2	901	250	4	3	64.36
Pakistan	1972/73	4	8	–	265	107	1	1	33.13
South Africa	1969/70	4	8	–	258	74	3	–	32.25
West Indies	1968/69	9	14	1	1196	242	5	6	92.00
Total		75	125	14	5357	250	33	15	48.26

Bowling

Opponents	Debut	M	Ball	Mdns	Runs	Wkts	Avrge	5	Best	Stk/Rt	RPO	Eco/Rt
England	1965/66	37	1839	44	730	26	28.08	–	4/34	70.73	2.38	39.70
India	1967/68	10	312	8	146	2	73.00	–	1/20	156.00	2.81	46.79
New Zealand	1973/74	11	494	8	245	9	27.22	–	4/39	54.89	2.98	49.60
Pakistan	1972/73	4	144	5	49	–	–	–	–	–	2.04	34.03
South Africa	1969/70	4	258	6	145	5	29.00	–	2/16	51.60	3.37	56.20
West Indies	1968/69	9	248	8	110	7	15.71	1	5/66	35.43	2.66	44.35
Total		75	3295	79	1425	49	29.08	1	5/66	67.24	2.59	43.25

Chapter Thirteen

A Case of No Balls?

Have we reached a sort of no-ball crisis? In the 1992–93 Sheffield Shield season bowlers forced umpires to urgently clear their throats about 700 times!

No-balls are worth one added to the score, or any runs the batsman might hit from the bowler's free offering.

In some first-class cricket they're now worth two added to the score, because administrators, alarmed by the ever-increasing carelessness of bowlers, decided that a 100 percent increase in the penalty would be a deterrent. It hasn't worked.

The problem with so many no-ball calls is that it slows the game down in an era when most people are using the fast lane. Observers are divided about the value of a return to the old 'back foot' rule and the merit of the newer 'front foot' rule.

The old rule said, in brief:

> *"The bowler shall deliver the ball with one foot on the ground behind the bowling crease."*

Its advocates maintain it enabled an early call, thus allowing the batsman long enough to aim a mighty, crowd-pleasing swipe.

The new rule says:

> *"The Umpire at the bowler's wicket shall call and signal "no ball" if he is not satisfied that in the*

154

delivery stride:-

(a) the Bowler's back foot has landed within and not touching the return crease or its forward extension

or

(b) some part of the front foot whether grounded or raised was behind the popping crease."

Many feel this is a fairer rule, especially with so many fast bowlers around these days. But is it best for the game as a spectacle?

DAVID GOWER

I have earlier extolled the satisfactions of being able to play the game of cricket to some sort of standard, but there comes a time for all of us when the playing of the game takes second place to talking or writing about it.

Lovers of the game all over the world have been discussing its finer and broader points for a long, long time, while the professional pundit explores exactly the same avenues, perhaps with a degree of extra knowledge, and with the added benefit of being paid for it, safe in the knowledge that for so many of the issues that vex the cricket watcher's mind there is no real right or wrong answer. Not only that, there are always plenty of issues to discuss, whether in the tavern or on print, some of which I am duty bound to air again here.

The administrators of the game are constantly seeking to maintain the viability of the product, to keep interest and therefore returns at the gate high. Hence a continuous process of tinkering with the laws and regulations, always with the supposed interests of the paying public at heart.

Currently high on the list of major concerns are the rules concerning bouncers and no-balls. As a mere willow wielder the row over front or back foot no-ball laws seems to have wasted far too much time and energy. Surely it is so simple for everyone to know exactly where the front foot must land, rather than setting up discs and the like as suggested by proponents of the back-foot law. Bowlers complain that the front-foot law gives them little margin for error, but I'd say the reason no-balls have plagued scorers and umpires so much recently is that bowlers have simply tried to cut that margin to the bare minimum too often.

Now that the penalty has increased to two runs given away plus whatever comes from the bat, we, now at the start of the English season, have already seen the number of no-balls reduced. I hope this trend will last all season and beyond; it proves that bowlers can work within the parameters set for them if properly coerced.

TONY GREIG

Under the existing no-ball law, some portion of the front foot must be behind the front line (popping crease)—and that seems very fair to me when one considers the other sports that have similar problems to cricket. Consider too how fast bowlers have abused the alternative over the years.

Olympic long-jumpers are required to jump from behind the line. If they overstep the mark the jump is not counted

> *Tony Greig was the first England player to score a century and take five wickets in a Test. Against the West Indies at Barbados in 1973–74 he scored 148 and returned 46–2–164–6. He also caught Gary Sobers for a 'duck'. In the Test 99 no-balls were bowled—a record!*

and after three 'no-jumps' they are disqualified. Surely, when one considers that long-jumpers run 70 metres in about seven seconds and are still expected to take off behind a given line and execute a jump or even a triple jump, we are entitled to ask our bowlers to stay behind the popping crease.

Some fast bowlers of yesteryear abused the previous liberal law and on occasions let the ball go from about a metre closer to the batsman than is now permitted. I am not at all surprised that my dad thought the bowlers of the forties, fifties and sixties were not only better, but quicker than Thommo and Lillee.

I don't think I would have been able to find 11 Englishmen to play against those two bowling from 18 metres. For the record the pitch is 20.12 metres wicket to wicket. The batsman normally stands one metre in front of his stumps, the bowler, under the present law, lets go from one metre in front of the stumps at the non-striker's end.

I don't think there is a sustainable argument against the fairness of the existing no-ball law, and unless an acceptable definitive alternative can be found which prevents the bowlers from getting any closer to the batsmen in delivery, we should stick with the existing law.

The only alternative I can think of is to use a disc which the umpire could place in position. The position of the disc would vary for each bowler and would depend on the stride and drag of the bowler.

Umpires obviously find the fractionally reduced time they have to look up from the popping crease and focus on the action disconcerting, but this is a *minor* problem by comparison with overstepping.

Perhaps umpires should exercise a little more flexibility in the interpretation of the existing law by warning rather than calling a bowler who oversteps by a centimetre every now and then. Umpires who have played first-class cricket seem to implement that degree of flexibility that is required to keep everyone happy.

BILL LAWRY

The high number of no-balls these days in Test or any international cricket has caused a lot of concern for everybody who hopes for an entertaining day and a good contest. Many players including myself believe that the old back-foot law gave the batsmen a split-second more time to have a free hit at the no-ball.

That means the bowler pays a higher penalty for bowling a no-ball. But modern cricketers, who have been brought up under the new front-foot law, are quite happy; they concede the law is there to stop the bowler getting a wicket off an illegal delivery, knowing it's unlikely they'll pay any run penalty as well. Surprisingly, modern umpires are quite confident they can judge other decisions like leg before or a caught behind despite having to look at the front-foot line and then look up sharply to make any decision. I think the time lapse between the two eye movements is not long enough to allow proper focus. The poor standard of umpiring in recent times supports my view.

Another aspect of the new rule is that the fast bowlers sometimes bowl a professional no-ball in order to intimidate the batsman by bowling closer to him. They know the ultimate penalty is just one run conceded and not the four or the two or the three that may have been the case under the back-foot law when the batsman had more time to have a free swing.

Spectators are being robbed of entertainment. The no-ball in modern cricket has become one of the most boring parts of a day's play. The bowler runs in, bowls a no-ball, nothing happens; there's no extra effort by the batsman because on most occasions he doesn't have time to play a shot unless it's a very bad delivery. One run goes up on the scoreboard and there's an extra ball to be bowled in the over.

Gone is the rush of adrenalin for the spectator who used to see a big swing from the batsman, maybe see a catch go to a outfielder, jump up in his seat and shout, "That's out!"— then when he sees the umpire's arm go out indicating a no-ball, relax. Great fun. It is very doubtful that this front-foot law will be changed, because it's been in for some time, but I'm not convinced that it is in the best interests of cricket as a game.

At some stage it would be worth a trial in some competition to revert to the back-foot law and see how modern umpires and players respond.

GREG CHAPPELL

I believe no-balls are a blight on the game and I'm not sure that the current no-ball law is doing the job adequately. Most good umpires are good umpires because they are flexible individuals, they have a reasonable sense of humour and they understand the frailties of human nature and fast bowlers in particular.

By strictly adhering to the letter of the law the umpires, I believe, are adding to the problem. If the bowler is overstepping the mark by a metre or two then obviously it's going to make a difference, particularly if he is a fast bowler, but a centimetre or two is not going to make a difference.

I think the situation can be improved. There is a lot of argument for the reintroduction of the back-foot law and that may well be an answer to the problem by allowing the umpires to give the bowlers a little more leeway.

I believe the back-foot law could work if the umpires have a marker which they put down for each bowler. The marker can be adjusted depending on the length of stride for each individual. This overcomes a number of problems.

Psychologically the bowler aims to land somewhere around the back line but if he puts a little bit of extra effort into it he is going to no-ball by a centimetre or two. By having the marker before the back line the subconscious focus of the bowler will be more to that marker. If that marker is anything up to 10, 15, or 20 centimetres behind the back line, the bowler is unlikely to overstep the front line. It allows a little bit more leeway for the bowlers because

> *The Chappells, Greg and Ian, were the first to score centuries in the same innings of a Test—113 and 118 against England at the Oval in 1972.*

their stride is going to change from time to time.

It also allows more time for the umpires to call no-ball and in turn allows more time for the batsman to take full toll of the no-ball. If I had a choice I would suggest that rather than alter the legislation that stands, the umpires should be encouraged to be a little more lenient—don't worry about an over-step of a centimetre or two.

But if they really wanted to get serious about solving the problem, then I think the system of markers would be one way of overcoming it.

IAN CHAPPELL

By returning to a common sense approach back-foot no-ball law, the administrators could improve over rates, the standard of umpiring and the entertainment value, and reduce to a minimum the number of no-balls.

It wouldn't, as most administrators seem to think, mean a return to the bad old days of dragging, where bowlers delivered from around 18 yards.

Chapter Fourteen

Back to Bodyline?

One of cricket's toughest calls is on fast bowlers. It's a riddle, "Define gross ignorance ..."

The answer, according to some particularly brave opening batsman, is, "A room filled with 144 fast bowlers."

Of course it does most fast bowlers a grave injustice. There haven't been too many dumb ones over the years, even though some followers of the game question the sense in anyone running 20 metres at full tilt on a stinking hot day, pounding down ball after ball at top speed.

And, despite a few celebrated claims to the contrary, most fast bowlers don't get enthusiastic at the sight of a bloodied batsman.

Oh, they like to hear the dullish thud of a ball's impact on the rib cage now and again, followed by the rush of exhaled air as the batsman doubles up, but that is all in the accepted softening up process.

Often the fast bowler would throw down a few bouncers every couple of overs—as a general rule three every two overs was the norm—just to keep the batsman on his mettle, even try to get him caught on the hook shot.

Now it's not that simple. Before he takes the field a fast bowler almost needs to make a quick call to his lawyer to check out just what he can do.

The rules on short-pitched bowling now take up a page in the book of laws.

Law 4.8 The Bowling of Fast, Short Pitched Balls

Experimental Regulation for Test Matches only for three years with effect from 1 October 1991.

"The bowling of fast short pitched balls is unfair if, in the opinion of the Umpire at the Bowler's end, it constitutes an attempt to intimidate the Striker, see Note (d).

Umpires shall consider intimidation to be the deliberate bowling of fast short pitched balls which by their length, height and direction are intended or likely to inflict physical injury on the Striker. The relative skill of the Striker shall also be taken into consideration.

A bowler shall be limited to one fast, short-pitched ball per over per batsman. If this limit is exceeded, the following procedure shall be applied:-

(a) If a bowler delivers a second fast, short-pitched ball in an over to the same batsman, either Umpire shall call and signal "no-ball" and indicate the reason to the bowler, to the Captain of the fielding side and to the other Umpire.

(b) If a bowler is no-balled a second time in the innings for the same offence, the Umpire shall warn the bowler, indicate to him that this is a final warning and inform the Captain of the fielding side and the other Umpire of what has occurred.

(c) If the bowler is no-balled a third time in the same innings for the same offence, the Umpire shall:-

(i) as soon as the ball is dead, direct the Captain of the fielding side to take the Bowler off forthwith and to complete the over with another Bowler provided that the Bowler does not bowl two overs, or part thereof, consecutively;

(ii) not allow the Bowler, thus taken off, to bowl in the same innings;

(iii) report the occurrence to the Captain of the batting side as soon as the players leave the field for an interval;

(iv) report the occurrence immediately after the day's play to the Executive of the fielding side and to the governing body responsible for the match, who shall take any further action which is considered to be appropriate against the bowler concerned".

Delete Note (d) and insert the following:

"A fast short pitched ball shall be defined as a ball which passes, or would have passed, above the shoulder of the batsman standing upright at the crease."

The 'Bodyline Tests' of 1932–33 stick in the memory as the time short-pitched bowling was nothing more than over-the-top intimidation of batsmen.

Nothing has really approached it since, despite the presence of Lindwall and Miller, Tyson and Statham, Heine and Adcock, Lillee and Thomson, and take your pick of Holding, Roberts, Garner, Marshall, Croft, Ambrose, Walsh and Patterson.

But still the rule-makers worry there could be an encore, and continue to re-programme the attack mode allowable to fast bowlers.

The question is: has the decision to allow a fast bowler one bouncer per batsman per over had a less desirable effect on the game than the one intended—to reduce the amount of short-pitched bowling?

BILL LAWRY

The new bouncer law has been brought about by the dominance of the West Indian team over the last 15 years with their army of fine fast bowlers of the calibre of Andy Roberts, Joel Garner, Michael Holding, Curtly Ambrose and company.

Unfortunately, the law change has done nothing to alleviate what could be, at any time from any bowler, ruled intimidation. All it has done is cause tremendous confusion among umpires worldwide as to what is a genuine bouncer.

It has made life very different for those batsmen who welcome the short-pitched delivery so they can play hook or cut shots, because now they might only get one or indeed no bouncers bowled to them during the course of an over. And, of course, it has taken away from the great fast bowlers one of their strongest weapons—a genuine bouncer at the right moment to a batsman who may not be capable of playing a horizontal bat shot like the hook.

The people that make these laws missed the point. They felt that the bowling of too many bouncers per over was taking away the effectiveness of a batsman and his ability to score enough runs per over to make Test cricket an interesting contest. But what it has brought about now is the fact that fast bowlers—particularly the West Indian bowlers of the tremendous calibre of Curtly Ambrose—can now intimidate batsmen with short-pitched deliveries which indeed are not bouncers.

Law 42 gives the umpires plenty of scope to warn bowlers who actually intimidate batsmen. The law clearly states that batsmen's calibre and position in the batting order should be taken into consideration. Fast bowlers who went outside the genuine spirit of the law could be controlled.

The unfortunate part about law 42 was that umpires didn't, or wouldn't, enforce it, mainly because, one feels, they didn't think they would be backed up by administrators when bowlers were either taken out of the attack or reported for intimidating batsmen.

There's no doubt that the new bouncer law is not working—it is causing a lot of problems for umpires and bowlers and indeed causing bad feeling between sides.

Batsmen now stare at umpires when a ball may go just

over their shoulder and the umpire hasn't interpreted it as a bouncer and the no-ball is not called.

The sooner officials worldwide go back to law 42 and force the umpires to use that law correctly, the sooner the problem of intimidatory bowling will be stopped. There's a big difference between great fast bowlers bowling bouncers to top-order batsmen and great fast bowlers intimidating lower-order batsmen with balls delivered at their throat or chest.

TONY GREIG

For over 100 years the old intimidation law worked perfectly well. Under this law, it was up to the umpires to decide whether or not fast bowlers were intimidating the batsmen. The persistent bowling of short-pitched deliveries, especially to those who could not bat, tailenders, was frowned upon. Warnings were issued, and then the bowler was removed from the attack for that innings if he chose to ignore the umpire's call for restraint.

Then, in the late seventies helmets for batsmen were introduced, and for mine that has changed everything relating to intimidation.

Helmets meant a batsman could take one on the head from Lillee and then, still standing, be in a position to tell him to "get nicked". It used to be that a blow to the head was what we all worried about—then suddenly there was no need to bother worrying anymore!

There is little likelihood that the batsman will get killed by one of those sickening thuds to the head we experienced from time to time when men were men!

Let's get back to the old law as soon as possible and instruct umpires to interpret it more flexibly than was previously the case. This will also stop tailenders blocking endlessly, knowing they can receive only one bouncer an over. The tailenders may even revert to batting the way they used to bat—get on with it or get out!

Tony Greig's 110 in the First Test at the Gabba in 1974–75 was the first for England at Brisbane since 1936–37. He did so in the face of Australia's fieriest fast bowling pairing since Lindwall and Miller—"if Lillee don't get ya, Thommo must!" was the crowd's laughing slogan.

The hook and pull are both great shots to watch, but the ball has to be short for the shot to be played—let's encourage it!

The 'old law' 42.8 states: "The bowling of short-pitched balls is unfair, if in the opinion of the umpire at the bowler's end, it constitutes an attempt to intimidate the striker.

"Umpires should consider intimidation to be the deliberate bowling of fast short-pitched balls, which by their length, height and direction are intended or likely to inflict physical injury on the striker. The relative skill of the striker shall also be taken into consideration."

The wording of that law at least gave the umpires some leeway. But the Australian Cricket Board has added its experimental regulation saying: "A bowler should be limited to one fast short-pitched ball per over, per batsman. The fast short-pitched ball should be defined as a ball which passes or would have passed above the shoulder of a batsman standing upright of the crease."

I'm not going to comment on this attempt to be more specific about the short-pitched ball, other than to say that the current law, combined with the Australian rules and playing conditions, is ridiculous.

DAVID GOWER

Most batsmen who possess both ability and bravado would be quite happy for the pacemen who face them 18 metres away to pound the middle of the pitch as often as they like. Not many batsmen, myself included, actually want to spend half their time avoiding short-pitched bowling, but we do accept that such bowling is one of the options of an opponent blessed with the ability to make a cricket ball hustle through. On a good day we will happily take advantage of whatever scoring opportunities such bowling can also bring.

By limiting the number of bouncers that climb to a suitable height, the guardians of the game have reduced the chances of seeing a Viv Richards or Richie Richardson take on the challenge a bouncer attack presents. On the other hand, if you add up the chances available to play the hook, pull or cut in any substantial innings by batsmen of that ilk, there will still be enough opportunities for the bowler to test them out to see whether the ball will end up in long leg's hands or 18 metres back in the crowd.

There are of course many batsmen to whom the short ball is just something to avoid at all costs, and to the spectator the sight of a batsman constantly ducking beneath such balls is understandably less than fully entertaining.

I actually think the result has been a success, with many of the world's fast bowlers realising that bowling a fuller length often brings the results they were looking for initially—wickets in the bag. It is not as though the bouncer has been completely outlawed, though the feeling that some lesser batsmen are benefiting from an extra degree of protection is inescapable. Overall I would say that the likes of Ambrose, Wasim and Waqar have suffered little from the rule; all of them have had much recent success without resorting to bouncer wars. Indeed most batsmen would agree that the high bouncer poses less of a threat than the ball aimed at chest or throat height. I rest my case.

GREG CHAPPELL

I believe the new bouncer law is a cop-out by the administrators. There was enough in the previous legislation for the umpires to be able to keep control of the bouncer situation. A captain was not going to take the risk of losing one of his key strike bowlers if he was warned a couple of times for bowling bouncers or intimidating batsmen.

If the umpires had been prepared to stand up and be counted, and had they believed they would be supported by the administration, they could have taken a tougher line.

I don't believe the restriction of bouncers per over is the answer. Legislation doesn't allow for the human element and the human element is always going to find a way around legislation.

Frustration is going to build up among bowlers when they are bowling on a wicket that is not a great deal of assistance to them and they get warned for bowling more than one bouncer per batsman per over. That frustration is going to overflow and create other problems that umpires will have to deal with, such as an increase in incidents of backchat between batsmen and bowlers. So in the end the new law will exacerbate other problems and fail to solve the one it set out to.

IAN CHAPPELL

The most dangerous aspect of a bouncer is the uncertainty of when it might be delivered. By limiting the bowler to one per over, per batsman, the administrators have diminished the element of surprise to the point where the law is ridiculously in favour of batsmen.

A Test match is exactly that—a *test* of skill, courage and intelligence. The batsmen must be tested and the tailenders protected.

This latest piece of lunatic legislation has managed to do the impossible. It has united batsmen, bowlers, former players and umpires—they all think it's stupid.

Chapter Fifteen

Extras

Commentators are there to comment—simple. Our commentators have expounded on a range of cricketing controversies.

> *Richie Benaud on the state of cricket today*: "No more Test nations please!"
>
> *Greg Chappell on crowd behaviour*: "Streaking and the 'Wave' are mindless pastimes."
>
> *Bill Lawry on modern cricket*: "Do Test teams need a coach?"
>
> *Richie Benaud on women cricket commentators:* "I would like to see women trying out for commentators' jobs at the same time as men."
>
> *Greg Chappell on Queensland's Sheffield Shield failures*: "I know there wouldn't be too many teams anywhere in the world that have played in as many finals as Queensland have and not won."

RICHIE BENAUD

No more Test match nations please. We have nine now and there is hardly room for all the matches they want to play.

Test cricket started with England and Australia, then came South Africa, West Indies, New Zealand and India. This made up a nice even six-ball. When there was partition in India, Pakistan became the seventh nation and, in recent years, they have been joined first by Sri Lanka and then Zimbabwe.

There are no others immediately on the horizon, but you never know. Pity the poor administrators from all countries who are charged with the task of sorting out the programming, bearing in mind that Australia and England will continue to play their Ashes series every two years, with Australia touring England every four years.

The first excuse for losing that leaps to the lips of captains and players these days is that the team is playing too much limited-overs cricket.

Richie Benaud was on the field for two of Test cricket's slowest days, both Australia versus Pakistan, both at Karachi. On October 11, 1956, after Australia had been dismissed for 80, Pakistan had only advanced to 15 by stumps, Test cricket's slowest day. On December 8, 1959, in front of the American president Dwight Eisenhower, Pakistan scored 5/104 in the day, the second slowest day in Test cricket history. Eisenhower was the first US president to see Test cricket—he may be the last!

Well then, for heaven's sake, play less if that's what you want!

As it happens, limited-overs cricket is the lifeblood of the game in several countries but, if they want to test the market and earn the undying gratitude of the traditionalists, then give it a go. At the same time though, the tour guarantee for a visiting country would be reduced by, say, a million dollars, and the payments to players would be halved.

That's fine with me, and it will sort out those who really believe what they are saying and are not merely whinging about one-day or day-night cricket.

Looking at the Australian situation, the biggest difficulty lies in fitting in the required number of tours, and how do you do it. Let's take the last of the two nations mentioned earlier.

If they were to tour Australia either separately or together, common sense decrees in these modern times that, if they played a series of Test matches and no limited-overs Internationals, the tour could be a financial disaster, when you take into account the cost of air travel and accommodation, plus all the incidental expenses of the tour and payments to the players.

Or would everyone expect them to play for nothing? The only way to generate extra income would be to play a series of limited-overs Internationals but, if at the same time you are being told there are too many of those, what solution do you offer?

We do need to sit back and take stock of what can be done by way of programming before we start thinking about having any more than the present nine Test countries.

IAN CHAPPELL

It always amuses me that cricket is such a trusting game. Why for instance don't the umpires supervise the toss? They do in football.

I remember the first time I captained South Australia. Being the home captain I tossed and Tony Lock of Western Australia called "heads". The coin rolled on its edge for some metres and when I got there I discovered it was a tail. I fully expected 'Lockie' to be right next to me, but when I looked up he hadn't moved, so I said, "It's a tail Tony. Do you want to check it?"

"No son, I trust you," said Lockie, "but if it was Bill Lawry, I'd have been over there like a shot."

Nowadays, in international matches in Australia there's no need to have an umpire supervise the toss, because the Channel Nine cameras are always on hand.

Despite the microphone and cameras, the odd captain forgets himself when he loses a toss that he's obviously keen to win.

It's usually a minor expletive and, more often than not, muffled. However, Viv Richards did once let go with the dreaded four-letter expletive when he lost the toss. When I told Viv about it later he didn't even realise what he'd said.

I heard correctly on that occasion, but not so when Arjuna Ranatunga was captain of Sri Lanka.

Allan Border tossed the coin and Arjuna called. The coin

came down opposite to what I thought the Sri Lankan had called, so I started towards Allan. However, Arjuna said, "We'll bat."

When Allan didn't object I had to change tack and interview Ranatunga first.

The next time these two tossed, exactly the same thing occurred. I was bemused by this and later in the day I told Allan I thought he was being duped.

Allan was surprised when I told him, and he was adamant that everything had been according to Hoyle. So I went and listened to the tape of the toss. Hearing the recorded version didn't change my mind and one or two of the production crew agreed with me. However, the producer listened and immediately disagreed, saying that I was "a deaf bastard", because Arjuna had called correctly.

You wouldn't think that heads and tails could sound alike, but to my ears Arjuna made them sound very similar. Mind you, when I informed AB that he'd interpreted Arjuna's calls correctly, there was a suggestion from Australian team manager Ian McDonald that my head was up my tail at the toss.

GREG CHAPPELL

Streakers were a fad that came to cricket in the seventies, much like today's 'Wave', but thankfully on a smaller scale. Just about everyone laughed at the game's first 'official' streaker who by a remarkable coincidence had a name pronounced like Michelangelo, but spelt Michael Angelow.

He came on at Lord's in 1975 when we were playing England, and the publicity moved numbers of slightly unbalanced people, whether through alcohol or whatever, to follow the trend.

I had a run-in with a few of them, the most celebrated being one at Auckland in the 1976–77 season.

This bloke took all his clothes off and proceeded at first just to run up and down among the crowd, then sit down again. This went on for quite a while, yet the police seemed just to let him go. The next thing of course he's over the fence and streaking. All he had on was a set of headphones with the cord hanging loose down his front.

I got annoyed about this bloke interrupting the cricket and as he came towards the pitch I moved out to meet him, and extended my hand as if to greet him with a handshake.

I thought he might think I was supporting him, but my hidden agenda was to grab him and hold him until the police arrived.

But the police were making rather slow progress, so I finished up holding the streaker's hand for a lot longer than he wanted, and he announced he was going to stick something in my ear. What I'm not sure; it was either the headphones cord, or something else! So there we were out in the middle, me totally annoyed with this clown disrupting the game, and him trying as hard as he could to extricate his hand from mine.

In the end I was holding on tight with my right hand and belting him a couple of times around the backside with my bat, which I had in my left, just to get him to stand still until the police arrived.

In the end he had me charged with assault, but the local police chief saw it never got to court. The unfortunate upshot of all this was that I was run out off the very next ball bowled after the disruption.

A lot of people thought my concentration had been broken, but I just didn't hear the call from Rick McCosker. Rick hit the ball to mid-on and as I always did I watched the ball going to the fieldsman.

There was so much noise as the streaker was being escorted from the field that the call from Rick was drowned out, and by the time I looked back Rick was halfway down the pitch.

So in the end I suppose I paid the penalty for getting involved. It's not just the players who are affected—the public's enjoyment is too.

Streaking and the 'Wave' are mindless pastimes. The mess and the disruption to the game are something cricket can well do without.

BILL LAWRY

One of the big talking points these days among players, former players, the media and administrators is: do Test teams need a coach?

Australia's decision to appoint Bob Simpson back when the going was tough for our boys, when the rebel teams went to South Africa about the mid-eighties, has been very successful, and has led other nations to make similar appointments.

Touring teams no longer have a manager and an assistant manager. I'm sure in the past when ex-players like Ken Barrington and Alec Bedser managed England teams they were in some ways filling a coaching role, they just weren't tagged 'coach'.

I think the role of the Test captain is so extensive today, with the amount of cricket being played and the greater media interest, that he does need an assistant.

To what extent, or in what area, he receives assistance is I guess up to the captain, but it would be disappointing if we ever reached the stage where modern players weren't doing the basic fundamentals right. By that I mean running between the wickets, fielding and throwing more than whether the left foot is in the right place for a forward defensive shot.

What I would stress is that the captain has always got to be in control. At the end of the day the captain is the one who has to make the decisions on the field, so he's the one who'll be copping the flak.

Of course the coach has to be capable, and that raises for me another query. Just how many of the coaches around would be capable of coaching at Test level? And, if the position is put out to tender, what are the qualifications of those making the appointment?

Coaches at this level have to be careful not to stereotype players; you want them to be natural, to display their God-given talent. Cricket has survived as a unique game.

Some players who appear to have ordinary techniques have survived at the highest level. They are the freakish

Opening batsman Bill Lawry carried his bat through the innings twice when playing for Australia in Tests: he made 49 not out in 107 against India at Delhi in 1969–70, and 60 not out in Australia's 116 against England at Sydney in 1970–71.

players who defy the coaching manual and who can not only win matches by themselves on occasions, but can also be great crowd entertainers.

If we coach them out of the game we'll finish up with a very dull, boring product. Administrators should always be aware of that—there will always be a few 'Dougie Walters' coming through in among the pure talents like Greg Chappell and Dennis Lillee.

DAVID GOWER

Ian Chappell has already named his team of 'tough guys'. Chappell was a tough guy himself, never inclined to take a backward step, and it was generally accepted he was able to inspire similar intestinal fortitude among the players under him. So it seems just as natural for me to select an XI of left-handers whom I have played with or against during the period of my career. You will note that I have picked a side that comprises left-handed batsmen: if they happen to bowl more than usefully with their right arms, so much the better!

I have started with *Mark Taylor* and *Brian Lara*, one steady and productive, certainly against England, and the other typically Caribbean, flamboyant yet productive—just remember the SCG, New Year 1993.

Alvin Kallicharran at No. 3 might just jog a few memories of one of the smaller West Indians, who made up for any lack of inches in height by playing the hook rather well, even to the likes of Dennis Lillee, who was not averse to testing that ability in a batsman.

My boyhood hero comes in at No. 4, *Graeme Pollock*, whom I saw score a Test hundred at Trent Bridge when I was eight, another hundred at Port Elizabeth when I was 17, and yet another when I played alongside him in Newcastle some years later. Now he could really play!

Allan Border I've admired both as a player and a friend. As the world's greatest accumulator of Test match runs he gets in just before the most successful West Indies captain of all time, Clive Lloyd. Not a bad duo in the middle of the order, with the best part of 18,000 Test runs between them.

At No. 6 is the greatest allrounder of all time, *Sir Garfield Sobers*, another boyhood hero, whose career just overlapped mine. For good measure, and in the light of the spirit of enjoyment he maintains in his sports to this day, he is also the captain of my XI. At least we should see some entertaining cricket played by this team.

Next comes another knight, *Sir Richard Hadlee*. He could bat and bowl a bit, and still holds the world record for Test wickets, which is plenty good enough for me.

Currently one of the most devastating bowlers in the world, and a little low in the order at No. 9, at least in a normal team, comes *Wasim Akram*. I am sure he can be just as effective without Waqar Younis at the other end, especially in this team.

My wicketkeeper, also very low in the order for a scorer of a Test match hundred, is *Rodney Marsh*, another very likeable fellow and a top performer with the gloves.

Last and certainly not least is *Curtly Ambrose*, very tall,

very quick, and above all very good. He is the sort of man who makes you wish that if you were going to have to play Test cricket, perhaps you would've been better off born West Indian so that you could play alongside him, not against him.

This is a side that would score its runs at the right sort of pace to give itself a chance to bowl the opposition out in time. And just in case you think I am light on spinners, I just thought that Sobers, Border, and even Kalli could chip in if necessary. But bear in mind that you would hope an attack like this might not need the twiddlies too often!

GREG CHAPPELL

The most common question I'm asked is: why haven't Queensland won the Sheffield Shield? It's a tough question to answer. I know there wouldn't be too many teams anywhere in the world that have played in as many finals as Queensland have and not won one.

In the early and mid seventies when I first transferred from South Australia I think we did have teams good enough to win the Shield. But the weather got in our way on one occasion and in 1973–74 it was a tornado-like bowling performance from Jeff Thomson that sank us.

They were the times of bonus points for first innings batting and bowling performance, and to beat Victoria for the Shield we had to gain 15 points from the last match against NSW. From memory we got about half a dozen, a miserable amount, mainly because Thommo took seven wickets.

You can see the great irony in that—Thommo later switched to Queensland and now he's the coach.

If hard luck via the weather played a part in past disappointments, these days it's the pressure of never having won the Shield that seems to be dragging Queensland down. It's hard to underestimate the pressure of playing in a Shield final when you're on the team that has never won after 60 attempts.

People just never let up asking "Is this the year?" No other team has to put up with that sort of relentless pressure. Tasmania is the only other State not to have won the Shield, but they've only been around a short time.

Queensland have often been criticised for playing so many imports and who knows, maybe it is a blessing in disguise that they were unable to win with overseas players like Majid Khan, Alvin Kallicharan, Viv Richards and so on.

If they had, the administration might still be pursuing that line instead of trying to bring on home-grown talent, which is the aim of today's administration.

Queensland's chief executive Barry Richards understands the need to build depth in Queensland cricket, starting by sorting it out at junior level then having it filter through to senior level.

Queensland produced some outstanding cricketers through the fifties and sixties. Names like Peter Burge, Wally Grout and Ken Mackay spring to mind. The State has always had a great deal of junior talent and has won as many of the youth competitions as any other State over the years.

But it seems that along the way they lose that talent somewhere, because there doesn't seem to be the continuation into the senior ranks. It may even be right to say there is not the depth of commitment in Queensland that there is in some of the larger States.

I don't know what puts them off the game, perhaps it's the hot humid climate. And I dare say the proximity of the beaches, up or down the coast, might be a contributing factor in any decision of whether or not to stand under the hot sun for a few hours at a time.

If Queensland could win the Shield with a basically home-grown outfit, I think that would have a very positive effect on keeping more young people in the game.

Queensland has always been able to provide players for the Australian team, but the recent selection of Matthew Hayden is sure to be a further spur to youngsters to take on the game. There are others in the wings, Martin Love, James Maher and the very promising fast bowler Michael Kasprowicz.

I believe, in time, Queensland's home-grown talent will once again be the force in Australian cricket it was back in the days of Burge, Grout, Mackay, the Archer brothers, Ron and Ken, and Don Tallon.

And, of course, they'll win the Sheffield Shield!

BILL LAWRY

I guess when you play first-class cricket for nearly 20 years and you have a physical feature that stands out as much as my nose does, then you have to expect some attention from the cartoonists.

My scrapbook, not that it is very big, is filled with cartoons of a long nose covered in cobwebs, grinding out the runs, which I thought were just fantastic.

If you are going to play any kind of sport, you have to have a sense of humour, have to be able to laugh at yourself, in fact that applies to life itself.

Now I'm on the commentary team when I go to the ground there's a sign up, "Bill Lawry's hanky", which covers about two bays at the great Melbourne Cricket Ground—you have to have a chuckle, and enjoy it.

Crowds love their signs, more so today because of television, and that has led to a drop-off in what were, when I was playing, some of the funny comments from the outer.

I'd be battling along and I'd hear, "You'll never die of a stroke, Lawry!" which was very funny. Comments like that from spectators can sometimes break up a tense situation, or a boring situation, or even a frustrating one if you can't get the ball off the square because the bowling is so good—as it probably was in this instance!

Maybe it's because of the professionalism of the game these days that players have lost their sense of humour.

Cricket has had some great personalities, like Max Walker and Merv Hughes, who have got the crowds on side, but you don't see too many smiling first-class cricketers today. It's their full-time living and they are very intense about it.

It's a tough environment, working hard pre-match, during the match and after—full-on all the time. A case of "stop laughing, this is serious".

The crowds entertain themselves these days, particularly the one-day crowds, where the wit of the banner has taken over from the wit of the verbal barracking.

I'll never forget the time at the Gabba when the crowd put the pig over the fence with "Botham" penned in big black letters on its side.

That brought the house down. And just as funny was the time Jenny Craig's phone number went up, paging "Mike Gatting". Then there was the time at the MCG when Greg Chappell was in the middle of his dreadful run of ducks and they let a rabbit and a duck onto the field.

How they got them in I'll never know. In a bag I suppose. The rabbit ran off down a drain but the duck continued out onto the field, which I, with my warped sense of humour, thought very funny given Greg's predicament.

Of course I wasn't the one having the run of ducks!

Some of the crowd behaviour these days is a pity, and has taken away a lot of the fun of days gone by. The media tends to focus on the drunks and the riots and bad crowd behaviour worldwide.

But really a vast majority of cricket fans have a great sense of humour. You see it every time you go to a game, and see their slogans hanging from the grandstand railings, whether it's a comment on some player, a commentator, or just a quote on life.

They should be encouraged. I think we should be having awards for the best slogans. That way people could go along not just to enjoy a great game of cricket, but to have a bit of a laugh during the match as well.

RICHIE BENAUD

"Why don't you have more women cricket commentators?" Give me 20 bucks for every time I've been asked that in the past 16 years and I'd be retired to some far-flung island. Why don't we have *any* women cricket commentators might be a better question than "more".

Channel Nine used Kate Fitzpatrick for a short time some years ago but I have always felt it was hardly a fair trial because, as she settled into her chair, she was surrounded by a mass of press photographers and journalists hanging on every word, or perhaps hoping for either a gem or an error. I wouldn't have enjoyed that any more than I expect Kate enjoyed it.

I would like to see women trying out for commentators' jobs at the same time as men and, at Channel Nine, they will receive the same courtesies as the men might expect. To me, the biggest problem will come when they are asked, as are the men, "What experience have you had in playing first-class cricket?" The obvious answer is "none" because of equally obvious circumstances.

There is no doubt that one of Channel Nine's strengths is that its commentators, whether they be ex-captains of national teams, ex-Test players, former or current first-class players, have the necessary experience to talk about a particular situation.

Viewers, in my experience, have a problem with accepting an opinion if it is not based on some form of experience. For example, much as I love golf and enjoy the golf work I have done, I am not prepared to offer an opinion as to why a top class professional golfer, say Greg Norman, has pushed a ball

Richie Benaud, on the 1953 tour to England, against T N Pearce's XI at Scarborough, hit 11 sixes and nine fours in scoring 135.

HOW DO YOU EXPECT ME TO BE
A COMMENTATOR IF I DON'T HAVE
ON-FIELD EXPERIENCE...!

to the right of the green. I'm quite prepared to say he *has* done it and describe what happened because that is fact.

I am a reasonably solid 10–handicapper at the Australian Golf Club in Sydney, and I know a certain amount about the game and the rules, but for me to add for millions of viewers that Norman hit the ball to the right of the green because his set-up was faulty, perhaps an inch or two too far to the left, he came off the ball a little, or he didn't allow for the slightly sidehill lie, would be, in my view, ridiculous.

It could just as easily have been that his grip was slightly faulty. I might be prepared to offer that type of commentary if later this year I were to pass all the PGA coaching certificate examinations, and if I managed to play in some big tournament events as an amateur so I could sample the intense pressure these players are under over the last nine holes on the final day, with a bunched leader-board and a first prize for the professionals of $200,000.

I am quite prepared though to offer praise or criticism of Allan Border's Test match captaincy, Mark Waugh's cover drive for four or dismissal, or why Craig McDermott was slanting the ball towards the batsman's pads. That's because I've been there!

IAN CHAPPELL

There's never a dull moment in the commentary box and I enjoy the work. It keeps you involved in the game in a way that you wouldn't be by just watching a day's cricket.

Working with other former players and a few current ones means plenty of variety. Not surprisingly, there's a divergence of opinions in the commentary box and these are often aired, which is healthy.

However it is important that commentators, while having the occasional disagreement, do work as a team.

This may sound strange, when Tony Greig and I so obviously disagreed a lot when we were opponents. However, I enjoy working with Tony and without the intensity of competition our disagreements are occasional and generally concern the relative merits of Australia and England.

Some people don't think it's possible for commentators to have a disagreement and then sit down together over a beer, a glass of wine or a meal at night.

As players we were all able to overcome a difference of opinion on the field to mix socially after a game, so I don't see why it should be so difficult after a day's commentary.

One of the reasons for the long-lasting success of the Channel Nine cricket coverage is the ability of the commentators to perform as a team while still retaining their individuality.

We're also fortunate in having a successful captain as our senior commentator. I believe Richie Benaud is the most knowledgeable cricket person around.

The Last Word

by Richie Benaud

Have you ever looked at someone you should know quite well, and been unable for the life of you to force the name through your lips?

The last Sheffield Shield match I played was in Adelaide and we had a great game against South Australia; I made a century as a farewell and then there was a cocktail party in the Association rooms, a very pleasant affair.

The speech was made by South Australian Cricket Association president Roy Middleton, whom I'd known for many years while captaining NSW and Australia. He made all the right noises and the theme throughout his speech was that here we had a man, about to retire, a man whose name is a household word, not only in Adelaide, but Australia, England, the world and possibly the universe as well.

When he asked everyone to rise to drink the health of this household name I suddenly took even more interest, because the whites of his eyes started to show as he was trying to remember who I was.

Eventually he managed the famous words "Richie Benny", which had all of us helpless and allowed Sir Donald Bradman the following week, before the start of the Sydney Test, to pin on the back of the dressingroom door a press clipping of a news story that the famous Jack Benny was to visit Australia.

On the top of the clipping in neat handwriting were the words, "Your brother I assume?"